"I often say it doesn't have to be perfect to be beautiful. Holley Gerth shows women that's just as true for our hearts as it is for every other area of our lives."

—**Myquillyn Smith**, The Nester, author of *The Nesting Place*

"In *You're Loved No Matter What*, Holley Gerth shares a breathtaking promise. She's not asking you to try to be better but inviting you to receive what's already yours. That's a message that will not only heal your heart but set you free."

—**Suzanne Eller**, international speaker and author of *The Unburdened Heart*

"If your heart feels entangled by the critical voices of perfectionism, sit down with this book full of encouraging gems of wisdom and let Holley's words guide you to a new beginning, to set your heart free to run in one direction: toward God's love for you."

—**Bonnie Gray**, author of *Finding Spiritual Whitespace: Awakening Your Soul to Rest*

You're
Loved
No Matter
What

Books by Holley Gerth

You're Already Amazing
You're Made for a God-Sized Dream
Opening the Door to Your God-Sized Dream
You're Going to Be Okay
What Your Heart Needs for the Hard Days
The "Do What You Can" Plan (ebook)
If We Could Have Coffee ... (ebook)
The Encouragement Project (ebook)

You're Loved No Matter What

Freeing Your Heart from the Need to Be Perfect

Holley Gerth

Revell

a division of Baker Publishing Group
Grand Rapids, Michigan

© 2015 by Holley Gerth

Published by Revell
a division of Baker Publishing Group
P.O. Box 6287, Grand Rapids, MI 49516-6287
www.revellbooks.com

Printed in the United States of America

Library of Congress Cataloging-in-Publication Data is on file at the Library of Con-gress, Washington, DC.

ISBN 978-0-8007-2290-6

In keeping with biblical principles of creation stewardship, Baker Publish-ing Group advocates the responsible use of our natural resources. As a member of the Green Press Initia-tive, our company uses recycled paper when possible. The text paper of this book is composed in part of post-consumer waste.

15 16 17 18 19 20 21   7 6 5 4 3 2 1

To My Heart Friends,
Who Love Me as I Am

Contents

Introduction

Here's the scandalous truth: we can be loved, accepted, happy, and less stressed *without* being perfect. Truly. As women, we tend to look at "perfection" as a superpower. If we could only be perfect, then we could beat depression, banish anxiety, and create unbreakable relationships. Being perfect feels like the best protection in a world that demands we have it all together.

But chasing perfection has hidden dangers. What we believe will lead us out of depression and anxiety may actually be part of what got us there in the first place. And the pursuit of perfection can keep us from discovering God's purpose for our lives. It can distort who he created us to be, and then the world misses out on the gifts only we have to offer.

Here's the reality: *you're not supposed to be perfect.* You're supposed to be human. And humans are messy, flawed, glorious, and deeply loved. Jesus already knows all of that about you. He can handle who you are. He doesn't expect you to be perfect. And if he doesn't, then you don't need to expect perfection from yourself either. Yes, when you read that it probably sounds a bit scandalous too. That's because many of us have believed twisted truths about what God wants from us. Please hang in there with me—I promise we will get to the doubts and questions that are probably popping into your mind right now.

For now it's time to lay down those unrealistic expectations that exhaust you.

It's time to embrace who you are—even the messy parts.

It's time to start living fully instead of just trying not to fail.

The pursuit of perfection keeps us from joy, love, peace, hope, and so many of the other gifts God intends for us. And here's the beautiful reality: you don't have to miss out any longer. Yes, embracing imperfection can be scary—especially when perfection has motivated us for a long time. But on the other side is freedom beyond what we could have imagined.

I speak about this from experience because I'm a recovering perfectionist. I know what it's like to trade law for grace and condemnation for love. And I'm more comfortable in my own skin and more in love with Jesus than ever before. Do I have it all together? Nope. And I'm okay with saying that out loud. Because I finally understand that I'm accepted anyway.

Let's stop trying to be perfect, friend. Instead let's be who God made us to be. Let's dare to live with joy. Let's embrace the freedom that is already ours through Jesus.

You don't have to be so tired anymore.

You don't have to live with a heart that's afraid.

You don't have to feel as if you're never enough.

Today can be a new beginning. Right here. Right now.

Are you ready?

Quick Quiz

Ways Your Life May Be Affected by the Pressure to Be Perfect

Place an X by each description you can relate to.

_____ **Isolation or Loneliness**—When we believe we have to be perfect, we may hide our true selves from others. Even when we're in a crowd, we can feel alone. We worry someone will discover "who we really are" and then we'll be rejected.

_____ **Anxiety**—Much of the anxiety we experience comes from worrying that we'll fall short of the expectations of others, God, or ourselves. If we don't live up to the standards we believe we must meet, then we become filled with fear.

_____ **Depression**—As we try harder to be perfect and it doesn't work, we begin to feel hopeless. And a loss of hope is at the heart of depression. We begin to feel weary and turn inward. We lose the desire even to make an effort anymore.

_____ **Irritability**—When we believe perfection is vital to our lives, the actions of others that don't line up with how we think things should be feel like a threat. We may lash out, seek to manipulate their behavior, or be very critical.

_____ **Indecisiveness**—If every decision we make has to be perfect, then it can feel impossible to decide what to do. Even small choices can become sources of fear, anxiety, and frustration. We may feel discouraged as our dreams or purpose seem to slip by, but we feel paralyzed when we think about taking action.

_____ **Low Self-Worth**—Every person has a different definition of what "perfect" even means. We all carry around an internal checklist of what we must do in order to be an acceptable human being. When we fall short, the way we feel about ourselves plummets as well.

_____ **Ongoing Physical Symptoms**—Our bodies aren't intended to bear the weight of perfection either. We may display our tension through frequent headaches, muscle aches, and fatigue. Our immune systems may be weakened in the short term and our overall health affected in the long term.

Why You Really Don't Have to **Be Perfect**

She walks into the room with a smile, but I can see the weariness in her face, so I ask her how she's doing. With forced cheerfulness, she declares, "I'm fine!"

After she sits down across from me, I lean in, look her in the eyes, and gently inquire, "Okay, how are you *really* doing?"

She sighs and shifts her gaze downward. "I'm worn out," she replies. "I'm tired of trying so hard all the time."

She tells me about all the pressure in her life. Whether it's her looks, her relationships, or even her faith, it seems there's always a standard to meet. She carries an impossible to-do list in her heart that never gets completed. She lives in fear of letting someone down and yet at times resents the very same people she's trying to please. Sometimes she fantasizes about running away from her "blessed life" just so she can have some peace. She says it's been this way as long as she can remember, and she doesn't know how to live differently.

I nod in understanding and think of how I've wrestled with the need to be "perfect" too. The struggle began in my teenage years when I realized there were expectations to be met in every area of my life—school, social relationships, and even spirituality. I learned to hold my true emotions inside and perform so that I would be accepted. On one particular day my boyfriend broke up with me, and I felt devastated. But I walked into my next class with a forced smile. Fortunately, someone loved me enough not to let me get away with it. A friend took me by the shoulders, looked straight at me, and said, "Holley, stop faking it."

That moment turned out to be life changing because of this: until then I didn't think anyone could tell when I was faking it. I had become an expert at going through the motions and trying not to let anyone down. I thought my performance had been believable. But now someone stood in front of me, cutting through the masquerade and saying, "It's okay to be real."

I desperately wanted to believe that truth. I didn't want to keep pretending, but I had no idea how to change. Even more than that, I was terrified that if I let my struggles and true emotions show, God would be disappointed in me. Fear held me back and held up the corners of my smile like strings on a puppet.

Although I made some progress, I never really figured out how to stop trying so hard in high school. By the time I graduated, I had come to believe I could never live up to the standards and expectations. So when I went to college, I took a chain saw to the pedestal I'd been placed on and completely rebelled. I made poor choices and ended up miserable. Then I truly felt trapped. I didn't want to be perfect, but I also knew my destructive way of living had to stop.

God began relentlessly pursuing my heart in that in-between place between law and grace. He sent people into my life who accepted me in all my brokenness. He caught me when I fell. He revealed the legalism and lies that had led me to this cage of desperation. I learned—or perhaps relearned—that walking with

Jesus is always first and foremost about a relationship. My heart had begun to heal.

Then I got married and began a career. In my midtwenties my husband and I decided to start a family. Only it didn't turn out the way we planned. Seven years of infertility and loss led me to struggle desperately for control of my life. I thought if I could just do everything right, then surely God would give me what I wanted. But he didn't. I fell into depression, and he met me again in that place. He showed me once more how hard I'd been trying to keep it all together. And in that season, I learned how love could hold me together even when my world fell apart.

God has continued to peel back layers of perfectionism in my life bit by bit. He's restored me in more ways than I even knew I needed, and he continues to do so. When I began working as a counselor and then a life coach, I discovered other women struggled with the need to be perfect too. And as I wrote about this on my blog as well as in books, I heard more of the same through comments and emails.

Here's the reality: I've yet to meet a woman who doesn't struggle with the pressure to be perfect. Even the ones who seem to have it all together. Maybe *especially* those who seem to have it all together. We are all in this battle, and we can help each other find victory. So on the day when yet another woman shared with me what I'd heard so many times before, I knew the time had come to write this book.

I reached across the table and touched her hand with newfound hope in my eyes. "You don't have to be tired anymore. Your life really can be different."

She looked up at me with a half smile. "I would love to believe that," she answered. "I think I'm too worn out to try anything else."

I smiled back at her and said, "Well, that's great news, because the first thing I want you to do is stop trying."

I'm saying that to you today as well, friend. Before you read one more sentence in this book, please pause and promise this one thing: you will stop trying to change on your own. Aren't you exhausted? Aren't you ready for a break? Then get off the treadmill of perfection. You have permission to do so. Because this book isn't about making yourself better. It's about learning to receive what's already yours. It's about knowing you're loved no matter what. It's about rest and grace and living in an entirely new way.

Yes, it's possible to overcome the trap of perfection. I can say with all my heart that I'm a freer woman today than ever before. I know who I am and what I'm called to do. My days are far more joyful. My anxiety is less than it's ever been. Yes, I will be in an ongoing process of healing until I get to heaven. I will have bad moments and messes. But that's okay. And I've discovered it's okay with God too. My life is not perfect, but it's better and fuller than it's ever been. Yours can be too. Truly.

Before we get free, we need to understand why perfection so quickly traps us in the first place. What makes us so willing to give up the wide-open spaces of grace?

The Lure of Perfection

We're drawn to perfection like a magnet. Our hearts feel the pull from the time we're little girls. The new school year began here yesterday, and social media sites filled with photos of kids in their "first day of school" outfits. I remember that ritual well too. Every bow, backpack, and pair of shoes had to be just right. We do the same as grown women, only now it's our homes, careers, or faith we hope are perfectly put together. It seems that desire for a flawless first impression never goes away.

As I think about why those "first day of school" outfits mattered so much, it seems many of the heart needs we experience as children remain even when we're grown-ups. We want to be accepted. We want others to think favorably of us. We want to be safe and avoid exclusion or hurt. I think at the root of every desire for perfection is simply this: *fear*. The way we battle fear as humans is through control. And being perfect is the ultimate expression of control.

The enemy knew that when he tempted Eve all the way back in the Garden of Eden. Every time I return to this story, I seem to discover something new about who we are as women. And as I did so today, this one phrase stood out to me: "You will be like God" (Gen. 3:5). The enemy spoke that false promise to Eve to tempt her. But why that line? He could have offered her many other things—riches, illicit pleasures, the chance to rule the earth. But he chose those words: "You will be like God." In other words, *you will be perfect*.

What Eve in her innocence didn't realize is that she already *was* perfect. Yes, she was human rather than divine. But she was complete and whole in every way (which is the true definition of biblical perfection—we'll get to that later). She didn't lack anything. And yet, in his craftiness the enemy was able to convince her that she did. Friend, he still does the same with us today.

So how is "being like God" different than being human? What was so appealing about that to Eve? What does God have that we want for ourselves? I think there are five core answers:

Complete control—God has infinite power. Nothing is impossible for him. He's never surprised. Unlike us, he can do anything he wants whenever he wants.

Absolute knowledge—God understands everything. He can fathom more than we can even imagine. He never has to figure out a problem or search for a solution like we do.

Rightful glory—God alone deserves praise and honor because he created all things. He doesn't require affirmation to soothe his insecurities.

Self-sustaining love—God exists in perfect community within the Trinity. He doesn't have a "black hole" of love within him that he needs to have filled by anyone.

Secure identity—God's character does not change. He is who he is now and forever. Nothing can change or reduce him.

When women wrestle with trying to be perfect, it's related to one or more of the core needs above. We are trying to "be like God" in ways he never intended for us. We usually do so not out of arrogance but out of fear. Let's take a look at how that might unfold in a woman's life.

Complete control—Rachel grew up in a chaotic environment, so she learned to take charge. Now that she's a grown woman, that tendency shows in how she runs her home. As long as the house stays absolutely spotless and everything is in order, Rachel feels safe. Sometimes she's weary of trying so hard, but any alternative seems far too frightening.

Absolute knowledge—Kate doesn't know what's going to happen in her marriage. She senses a distance from her husband and once came across some inappropriate sites on his internet log. She tells herself, "If I can just do everything right as his wife, then he won't leave." She wants to confront her husband but fears what might happen. So she plays the role of the ideal wife while she remains deeply lonely inside.

Rightful glory—Sarah learned early how good achievement made her feel. An A on a test or an extra point scored in a game earned her pats on the back from her peers and parents. It's not that she wants people to think she's awesome; it's just that she's afraid if she isn't, they won't think of her at all. So she focuses on winning in life, but a lot of times there's simply no joy in the game.

Self-sustaining love—Gloria has been meeting the needs of others for as long as she can remember. When the phone rings, she answers. When the committee meets, she volunteers. When the friend goes into crisis, she shows up. She thinks being needed is the same as being loved. If she ever said no or let someone down, then she'd be rejected. On the outside she still wears a smile, but on the inside she's beginning to worry about the resentment she feels.

Secure identity—Krista has always felt like a bit of a chameleon. She can drift into a group and quickly learn what it takes to fit in. She embraces the phrases they use, the places they shop, and the values they hold highest. She's lived in so many different places that this kind of adaptation feels like a necessity. But sometimes she wonders who she could really become if she stopped pretending.

We can all relate to one or more of the descriptions above. If you felt a poke of guilt as you read those, swat it away. That's just perfection trying to get at you. God knows we are human and our hearts are drawn to what's not best for us. There is no condemnation for us in Jesus (see Rom. 8:1), and that means we're free to be honest so we can find healing. With that in mind, *which of those scenarios do you relate to most? Why?*

_____

_____

The reality is, we all have a little bit of each of these women in us. We're all fallen, broken, and searching for ways to fill the voids in our hearts. Like I just said, God understands and he doesn't condemn us. He sees how easily we can be trapped by the very things we think will set us free. He knows that we're tempted to try to be perfect so that we feel safe. He also knows that perfection is impossible for us. That's why he sent Jesus.

Here's the paradox: while we're *not able* to be perfect, we also *must* be perfect to stand in God's presence. We're born into sin, and none of us goes through life without messing up. Even if you're a really "good" person, that's not enough. "For whoever keeps the whole law and yet stumbles at just one point is guilty of breaking all of it" (James 2:10). We don't have any hope of achieving perfection ourselves. So what does that mean? *We need Jesus to transfer his perfection to us because we can never be perfect on our own.*

When Jesus died on the cross, he took the punishment we deserved on himself and resolved our sin issue once and for all. That's why he said, "It is finished" (John 19:30). When we believe in Jesus as our Savior, we receive not only salvation but also a new identity. "I have been crucified with Christ and I no longer live, but Christ lives in me" (Gal. 2:20). Jesus takes your sin and gives you his perfection in return. This truth is the center of the gospel. Without it, Christianity is no different than other religions, which tell people to try harder and do more good so they can get into heaven. *You do not have to live that way.*

The writer of Hebrews describes what Jesus did for us this way: "For by one sacrifice he has made perfect forever those who are being made holy" (10:14). Through Jesus, we are given perfection that we could never have on our own. That's *positional* perfection, and it allows us to stand in right relationship with God.

Positional perfection can *only* be received. It can never be earned. When we try to do for ourselves what only Jesus can, we take the power out of what has been done on our behalf. God wants to set us free so our lives will no longer need to be about pursuing perfection. He wants us instead to be a people of grace, love, and joy.

You might ask, "But doesn't God care about what I do?" Yes, he does. And when we realize how much he truly loves us, we care more and more too. So there's a second part to perfection: it's the process of "being made holy" described in Hebrews 10:14. This simply means that throughout our lives, God wants us to become more like Jesus. At the same time, he also knows that the process will not be complete until heaven.

And God is the one who perfects us—we don't do it ourselves. Our role is to stay in close relationship with him. As we do so, the changes that need to happen in our lives naturally begin to take place. Jesus said he's the Vine and we're the branches. Our role is simply to stay connected to him. Ironically, we stunt our spiritual growth when we're focused on making ourselves perfect.

We will go into much more detail about what I shared above throughout this book. We'll also talk about specific verses like "Be perfect, therefore, as your heavenly Father is perfect" (Matt. 5:48) that can cause confusion about what God expects from us. But for now I want your heart to take hold of these two essential truths:

- You do not have to be perfect for God to love or accept you. When you receive Jesus as your Savior, his perfection is transferred to you, and you are in right relationship with God.
- Until you get to heaven, you will be in a process of being made holy by God (in other words, becoming more like Jesus). In the meantime, God wants you to focus on your relationship with him and not on changing outward behavior.

You may be wondering, "But what do I do when I sin?" You can simply go to God and say, "I was wrong, I'm sorry, and I'm ready to change. Will you please forgive me and help me?" Then move forward knowing God loves you just as much in your worst moments as he does in your best.

The enemy told Eve, "You can be like God through your own efforts." Eve bought into that lie, and the story of humanity changed for all of history.

Jesus says instead, "You can only be like me through receiving what I did for you." And when we believe that truth, our lives are changed for all eternity.

Let's Pause for a Minute

Maybe as you're reading this you're thinking, "I always believed being a Christian was about leading a good life." If so, you're not alone. A lot of people have done the same. But that's not what Jesus tells us. He offers us far more! You don't have to try to be a "good" person so hopefully you can get into heaven. Instead you can receive what God has done for you right here, right now. Simply tell him:

> Lord, I believe you died for me and you alone are my Savior. I ask your forgiveness for my sins. I receive all you have for me—including a new identity and a secure eternity with you! Amen.

If you prayed that for the first time, write today's date below, because it's now your spiritual birthday! And tell someone this wonderful news. This is a reason to celebrate!

Where Does Our Desire for Perfection Come From?

If it's not humanly possible to be perfect, why do we feel so strongly that it's what we *have* to do? The pressure to be perfect can ambush us from several different places. These are four of the most common:

Our hearts—God has "set eternity in the human heart" (Eccles. 3:11). In other words, there's a part of us that knows there's more than this world and we are not yet all we will be. We're aware of our sin and the ways we fall short. God places "eternity" within us so that we seek out a Savior. That's a good thing. But when we decide to try to perfect ourselves, that need gets distorted.

Legalistic authority figures—Whether they're parents, church leaders, teachers, or coaches, those in authority over us have a tremendous impact on our view of the world. When we believe we have to perform perfectly to be loved by these people, we can begin applying the same approach to other areas of our lives as well. Rather than becoming bitter, it's important to recognize these legalistic authority figures are probably even more trapped than we are by the lie of perfection.

Painful childhood experiences—When we encounter anything that hurts us as children, our natural response is to make sure it never happens again. So if our clothes got made fun of at school, we might try to have just the right wardrobe as a grown-up. If we got yelled at by a parent for our messy room, we may feel anxiety if our house isn't spotless. If a teacher treated us harshly, we may work overtime to please our boss. What helped us adapt as children can actually harm us in later life until we learn new patterns.

Personal triggers—Think about an area of your life where you feel the need to be perfect. As you think about what might be the source of that feeling, is there a specific memory that comes to mind? When did you decide that being perfect in that area would keep you safe in some way? It can help to identify your personal triggers for feeling pressure to be perfect.

Like we talked about before, perfectionism is ultimately about self-protection. Once we recognize the source of our wound, we can ask God to come and heal it rather than continuing to try to do so ourselves. Think about where your hurts came from, and talk to Jesus about it through this prayer:

Lord, I realize that I've been trying to be perfect in certain areas of my life. I'm doing that because I feel afraid deep down inside. I thought if I could be perfect, then I would be safe. I wouldn't be rejected or hurt. I realize now that's not true. I need your healing instead. I need you to be the Protector of my heart. Please give me the courage to believe I don't have to be perfect to be loved because your grace is enough for me. I want to learn to live in a new way. Amen.

Is there anything else you want to add to this prayer as you share your heart with God?

_____

_____

Perfection is the stuff of divinity, not humanity. Its weight is far too much for us. You've probably been trying to carry the burden of perfection for a long time. It's time to set it down and let it go. Can you picture yourself doing that now?

Close your eyes and imagine standing before Jesus. Place your perfectionism at his feet. What does your heart feel as you do so? What is Jesus saying to you?

_____

_____

Now imagine stretching out your hands to receive what Jesus has for you instead. What does he want to give you? Who does he say you really are?

_____

_____

From now on, when someone asks you how you are, you don't have to settle for "I'm fine." Your heart can answer with what it has longed to say for so long: *"I'm free!"*

Embracing the **Freedom** That's Already Yours

I sit cross-legged on my bed and type on my laptop. When I look up, my reflection in the mirror catches my attention. I smile as I see the woman I am today surrounded by reminders of the girl I was before. I'm home visiting my parents and writing in the same bedroom where I once dreamed about what life would be like "when I grew up." I think of other reflections that mirror has shown me—first days of school, touch-ups before dates, puffy eyes from shedding tears or laughing late into the night with friends.

I remember tilting my head from left to right as I looked into that mirror, hoping if I could find just the right angle, then I would finally feel balanced and beautiful inside too. I wanted to be perfect because perfect meant you were invincible.

I remember many conversations with my parents in front of the mirror too.

Can I stay out an hour later?

Can I borrow the car?

Can I wear this dress?

My mom and dad talked things through with me, and as the years went by they gave me more of what every teen needs—freedom. They knew I had to try out my little wings before I would be ready to leave the nest. I imagined for a moment what it would have been like if they had said, "Yes, you can go to the mall with your friends," and I said, "No, thanks. I'll just stay within the four walls of this room. It's safer here. I don't want to make mistakes or let you down." They probably would have responded, "Holley, you're supposed to grow up, and that means exploring the world. You need to make good use of the freedom we're giving you."

Yet as believers we often hesitate to embrace the freedom and grace God has given us. We're so afraid of making a mistake that we never take hold of all he has for us. We focus on being safe and staying on the straight and narrow so much that we miss out on doing what God truly wants—which is seeing us grow into all he created us to be. If you could hold a mirror up to your heart, the reflection should look different than it did yesterday, a week ago, or last year.

We tend to prioritize acting perfectly all the time, while God focuses on helping us live in the *freedom* that's ours through Jesus. Because that's the only way real growth happens. Growth is a messy process. We will make mistakes. We will fall down. We will take a few wrong turns. That's why we desperately need a Savior. But what's even more dangerous than messing up sometimes is staying the same year after year. That's not "perfection"—it's decay. All living things must grow. That includes you.

So what has God given you freedom to do so that you can grow? The answers to that just may surprise and delight you.

You Have Freedom to Make Mistakes

Gymnasts practice their routines over and over again. By the time they get to the world competition level, their performances are expected to be flawless. Yet Shawn Johnson hit what could have been a serious snag in her career at an important moment. She says in *Winning Balance*, "That day when I went up for the beam, I fell twice in the same routine. This, of course, is unheard of. If you fall, you fall. But normally you don't fall twice . . . especially in the event finals." Devastated and with more of the competition to go, Shawn walked back into the training gym to talk with her coach, Chow. He said, "Mistakes are mistakes. . . . Something was simply off." Then he added, "You know, things happen. Mistakes happen. But it's time to pick yourself up. You have another event."[1]

Shawn Johnson took her coach's words to heart and went on to finish competing that day. She eventually became an Olympic gold medalist. Her coach understood this: without mistakes, we don't get better. Shawn didn't intentionally sabotage her routine. She wasn't being rebellious. She was simply being *human*. There's a distinct difference between a mistake and a sin.

Mistakes help us learn.
Sin is a choice we deliberately make even though we know better.

Mistakes are done with innocence.
Sin comes from a heart that holds rebellion.

Mistakes lead to growth.
Sin leads to decay.

Not only *will* you make mistakes, but you *must* make mistakes. That's the way babies learn to walk, kids find out how to ride bikes, and grown-ups figure out how to find their way in the world.

As Shawn Johnson learned, the only way to stand tall is to accept that sometimes you will fall. When you make mistakes, God doesn't condemn you. He says what Shawn's coach did: "Pick yourself up. You have another event." You will hear that over and over until you're home in heaven. But sometimes we don't do what Shawn did. Instead we say, "I totally ruined everything. I've let down the people who loved and invested in me. I didn't meet the expectations. I'm not living up to my potential. In order to keep from being a further disappointment, I'm stepping out of the arena altogether." Then we live safe, mediocre lives and breathe big sighs of relief, because while we're not doing anything really great, at least we're not failing.

Listen, friend, that kind of thinking doesn't come from your heavenly Father. It comes from the enemy of your soul who would love nothing more than to see you stop using your gifts, strengths, and skills to make a difference in the world.

Because here's the secret: in the kingdom of God, as long as you're still fighting, you're winning. God doesn't hand out medals for performance. He hands out crowns for perseverance. The Olympics began in ancient Rome, and it's likely the apostle Paul had them in mind when he said, "Everyone who competes in the games goes into strict training. They do it to get a crown that will not last, but we do it to get a crown that will last forever" (1 Cor. 9:25).

Practice doesn't make perfect, because that's impossible this side of heaven. Practice makes a person who will *try again*, and that's what God desires. No matter how far or how often you've fallen, you can still get back up today. Can your heart hear the cheers as you do?

You Have Freedom to Say No

Mistakes can be scary, because we worry about letting other people down. But even more frightening can be saying no to the request or expectation in the first place. We often believe the lie that being perfect means putting on a performance that pleases everyone. God says instead, "You have permission to disappoint people." Sound scandalous? Yes, I thought so too when I first considered it. Yet when we look at the life of Jesus, we see this truth over and over. If we are to accomplish God's purpose for our lives, we must be able to say no.

We live in a world with millions of words. Yet out of all those syllables and sentences, two little letters seem to hold the most power: "no."

We fear "no."

We avoid it.

We misunderstand it.

But being able to say *and* hear no is essential to surviving and thriving, to loving and being loved, to following Jesus. Our living Word actually said no a surprising amount, and usually to what looked like excellent opportunities on the surface.

No to becoming King (see John 6:15).

No to offers of instant satisfaction, wealth, and power (see Matt. 4:1–11).

No to coming right away when Lazarus became deathly ill (see John 11).

It's the last one that causes me to pause most. The other two seem like simple spiritual choices. But the third? Someone Jesus loved was *dying*. Yet he said no when asked to come immediately and instead waited two more days. When he made that choice, it hurt the hearts of Mary and Martha.

> "Lord," Martha said to Jesus, "if you had been here, my brother would not have died." (John 11:21)

> When Mary reached the place where Jesus was and saw him, she fell at his feet and said, "Lord, if you had

been here, my brother would not have died." (John
11:32)

Two friends Jesus deeply cared about were essentially saying
to him, "If you had said yes, then we would not be hurting and
disappointed right now." Jesus felt the pain of·that "no" in his
humanity.

> When Jesus saw her weeping, and the Jews who had
> come along with her also weeping, he was deeply moved
> in spirit and troubled. (John 11:33)

Saying no hurts—even when it's God's will. Especially when we
have to say it to people we love and then watch pain that might
have been prevented enter their lives because of it.

It's remarkable to see how Mary and Martha responded in this
incredibly difficult situation. They wondered why Jesus didn't
make a different decision, they shared their disappointment, they
showed their grief. Yet they did something wildly courageous too:
they received the "no" without turning against the one who said it.

We wrestle with the same as believers in God and friends to
each other: Can we hear a "no" and still believe we're loved? Can
we reply with grace in the middle of our desire to have a different answer?

Real friends love your "no" as much as they love your "yes."

Mary and Martha received a "no" when they wanted Jesus to
come right away. But that "no" led to the resurrection of Lazarus—a
miracle beyond what they could have imagined when they first
asked Jesus to come.

I wonder if Mary, Martha, Lazarus, and Jesus embraced and
wept again when they were reunited. But this time the tears would
not have been from sorrow. Instead they would be the kind we
shed when we see how God can transform even a painful "no"
into a glorious "YES."

It's a divine mystery: when we say and hear no freely, we give God room to work, to amaze us, to give us back to each other again. And even when love says no along the way, it always leads us to a greater yes in the end.

Here's the secret: *you can deeply disappoint people while still deeply loving them.* Jesus didn't thwart the expectations of the people in his life simply because he didn't feel like doing what they asked or because he was asserting his "rights." He did so because he knew they couldn't see the big picture and what was ultimately best for them was very different from what they had in mind. He also understood that obedience supersedes satisfying those around us.

There will be people in your life—good people, God-loving people, kind and generous people—who will completely derail you from God's purpose for your life if you let them. That's not their intention. They're most likely even doing what they are because they love you. But you've got to say no anyway. And you will most likely feel guilty and like a no-good-very-bad-super-selfish girl when you do. That's not true, and those feelings, while quite uncomfortable, will not kill you. But saying yes just might steal the life God intends for you to live.

You have permission to say no. Say it with love. Say it with grace. Say it with kindness. *But say it.* Doing so doesn't make you imperfect—it makes you purposeful. And ultimately that benefits everyone around you as well.

You Have Freedom to Be Who You Are

Saying no helps you say a louder "yes!" to what matters most, which is being who God created you to be and doing what he has called you to do. As soon as you start pursuing your true identity and purpose, you can bet you'll hear a lot of opinions about what that means for you. So if you try to be perfect in the ways others think you should be, you'll find yourself continually changing who you are to meet someone else's standards.

These varying human definitions of perfect even apply to something as simple as spaghetti sauce. Howard Moskowitz was hired by a major brand to discover the "perfect" spaghetti sauce so that the company could beat their biggest competitor. Surely with a fabulous team, professional taste analyzers, and modern technology, Moskowitz would find just the right recipe. But it didn't work out that way. Here's what happened next:

> Working with the Campbell's kitchens, he came up with forty-five varieties of spaghetti sauce. These were designed to differ in every conceivable way: spiciness, sweetness, tartness, saltiness, thickness, aroma, mouth feel, cost of ingredients, and so forth. He had a trained panel of food tasters analyze each of those varieties in depth. Then he took the prototypes on the road—to New York, Chicago, Los Angeles, and Jacksonville—and asked people in groups of twenty-five to eat between eight and ten small bowls of different spaghetti sauces over two hours and rate them on a scale of one to a hundred. When Moskowitz charted the results, he saw that everyone had a slightly different definition of what a perfect spaghetti sauce tasted like.[2]

That's exactly the same problem we run into: *everyone has a slightly different definition of what's perfect.* Moskowitz did discover some patterns. For example, some liked chunky sauce and others smooth. But there wasn't ever an exact solution for everyone. The result of the project ended up being not one "perfect" sauce but a whole variety of really good ones that met different needs.

God loves variety too. He expresses that through each one of us. When we think of "perfect" in our culture, it's almost a synonym for "exactly the same." But God wouldn't agree. His definition seems to be more along the lines of "wildly different." Just take a look at how many kinds of flowers there are, how each sunset varies from the next, how every snowflake that falls is one of a kind. We look at "perfect" as fitting into someone else's mold. The perfect wife. The perfect mother. The perfect employee. But God says you're one of a kind. He wants you to become more of who he created you to be, not a copy of someone else.

You Have Freedom to Carry Less in Life

Even when we know who we are and what we're called to do, it's still easy to carry extra expectations with us. Sometimes when I speak at events, the organizers have women do scavenger hunts through their purses as a fun way to start the evening. A woman from the stage calls out random items: "four or more tubes of lipstick," "thirty-two cents in change," and "driver's license that's about to expire." The first person to find that item wins. Purses are pulled out from under tables, and in the chaos contents are thrown everywhere. Pacifiers. Calendars. Receipts. Wrappers. Tissues. Mirrors. By the time the activity is done, the table is covered with visual reminders of how busy and complicated a woman's life can be.

If you're like me, much of what would come out of your purse would be related in some way to trying to be perfect. I've gone through seasons when my calendar was full of things I felt obligated to do because it helped me meet some standard. My ever-present, ever-being-reapplied makeup is an attempt at our culture's version of beauty. The receipts I would have found might show purchases that were more about making an impression than what I really wanted.

Carrying all of that can begin to weigh a girl down. But Jesus walks up beside us and offers this instead: "Come to me, all you who are weary and burdened, and I will give you rest. Take my yoke upon you and learn from me, for I am gentle and humble in heart, and you will find rest for your souls. For my yoke is easy and my burden is light" (Matt. 11:28–30). Jesus wants us to trade our purses of "perfection" for a much lighter load instead.

He offers us security in place of striving.

Full hearts instead of full schedules.

Receiving instead of trying to buy our way to acceptance.

A local store has a "trade your purse" day once a year. No matter what shape your bag is in, you can bring it in and get credit so you can walk out with a new one. Inevitably, women walk out with lighter loads than before. It's interesting what happens when they do: their shoulders are straighter and they walk taller. Jesus offers us the same. We don't have to carry the expectations of others. We don't have to go through life slumped over because we always feel like we're falling short. We don't have to fill our lives with what will ultimately make us feel empty.

We can *carry less* when we become convinced we're *cared for* more than we can even imagine.

You Have Freedom to Ignore the Pharisees

When it came to giving people loads to carry that made their shoulders stoop and their hearts drag, the teachers of the law and Pharisees were the experts in Jesus's day. Instead of giving a purse, they would have given women a whole set of luggage. And in each bag would have been endless sets of rules, standards, and expectations. Jesus described the Pharisees this way: "They tie up heavy, cumbersome loads and put them on other people's shoulders, but they themselves are not willing to lift a finger to move them" (Matt. 23:4).

While we don't have official Pharisees in our culture today, we have plenty of self-appointed ones. Usually they focus on one area of life. For example, a home Pharisee might look down on anyone who doesn't vacuum every day. A work Pharisee might turn up her nose at anyone who dares leave the office on time. A church Pharisee might cling a lot harder to the specific human-made traditions of her denomination than the actual gospel.

These people can be powerful influences on us—especially for those of us who tend to be "pleasers" by nature. A few scolding words from a Pharisee can crush us, while a few words of praise can entice us to try even harder. The same was true in ancient Israel. The Pharisees weren't really liked. But they were feared and respected. So when Jesus said in the Sermon on the Mount that even the righteousness of the Pharisees wasn't enough (see Matt. 5:20), it would have caused a reaction. Author Larry Osborne describes it this way:

> Jesus... started out by saying, "Unless your righteousness surpasses that of the Pharisees and the teachers of the law, you will certainly not enter the kingdom of heaven."
>
> He ended by saying, "Be perfect, therefore, as your heavenly Father is perfect."
>
> Those two statements had to be incredibly disturbing to his listeners. There was no way they could be as perfect as their heavenly Father.
>
> And since the Pharisees were considered to be the most righteous of the righteous, surpassing them was also out of the question. They were doomed! I guarantee you, no one who heard Jesus that day thought, "I can't be as perfect as the heavenly Father, but at least I can surpass the righteousness of the Pharisees. Those guys are a bunch of self-righteous losers."
>
> No. They were stunned. They had to be thinking, "That's impossible!" Which was exactly what Jesus

wanted them to think. His goal was to point them to the cross. He wanted them to understand that they couldn't pull off their own salvation. He'd have to do it for them. And that's why he played the Pharisee card. He knew they'd be blown away.[3]

Finding a Pharisee to follow in different areas of our lives is tempting because it makes us feel like achieving perfection is possible. A lot of times we even create our own Pharisees. In other words, we admire someone to the point that we feel like we need to be exactly like them. "If only I could decorate like Martha Stewart, cook like Rachael Ray, and be as beautiful as Angelina Jolie." Then we end up following the image we've created of those folks instead of Jesus.

And if we're honest, we each have a bit of Pharisee within us. There's probably at least one area of our lives where we push for our version of "perfection." It might be the way we think a house should be kept, how children should be raised, or what a good employee ought to do. We publicly or privately create a long list of must-dos in that area. And we can make ourselves and others feel pressure to live up to those standards.

Jesus is the only one who can set us free from our pharisaical tendencies. He tells us, "You don't have to please the Pharisees," and even more importantly, "You don't have to *be* a Pharisee." He shows us that our lives are about love and not performance. He extends mercy rather than demands. So even when we fall short in the eyes of others, we can still be confident standing tall in his. And we can lift others up by offering them true grace rather than our personal guidelines.

You Have Freedom to Take Risks

Jesus said the Pharisees were like "whitewashed tombs" (Matt. 23:27). They looked good on the outside, but all the signs of life were missing, especially growth and moving forward. Perfectionism is the great paralyzer. It tells us that we shouldn't take a step, make a decision, or try anything new because it might not be just right. The basis of this for many believers is what I call the "God's perfect will" myth. Like the standards of the Pharisees, it does have an element of truth in it. But it misses the heart of what God truly intends.

The "God's perfect will" myth says this: "God has one perfect will for my life. It's like a straight path, and if I take one wrong step off it, then I've messed up everything."

What's the natural response if that's true? Stand very, very still. That's exactly what the enemy would like for you to do. Don't move forward. Don't grow. Don't try new things. Just wait for the rapture and hope you don't die of boredom first.

Yes, God does have a perfect will. But it's not like a straight path. It's more like a GPS route. God has destinations for our lives, yes, but he also understands there will be detours, wrong turns, and delays along the way. That means for us to discover God's will, we've got to get in the car and start going somewhere.

Paul describes the process of finding God's will this way: "Do not conform to the pattern of this world, but be transformed by the renewing of your mind. Then you will be able to test and approve what God's will is—his good, pleasing and perfect will" (Rom. 12:2). In other words, stop taking directions from the world and instead follow God's ways. And as you do, you'll figure out how to get where he wants you to go.

Test and *approve* are active words. They're experimental. They imply trying something and seeing what happens. If you're supposed to be perfect, then you don't feel the freedom to take risks. Every time you test something and it doesn't work out, you see it as failure and a source of fear. In contrast, God is more likely to see it as part of the growth process in your life. You've learned something new that will help you move forward in what he has for you. But perfection tells us we shouldn't even consider what we're learning because acknowledging it means admitting we've veered off the road we thought we had to follow.

I'm leaving for a road trip in a few days. My husband and I along with some friends will make our way to a new city. We know we want to end up in a particular place. But in many ways, that's not the point. What matters most to us is being together, building our relationships, making memories, and experiencing life. God loves taking journeys with you too. He's not the driver's ed instructor in the passenger seat giving us threatening looks if we even think about trying a new route. Instead, what matters most to him is being there with us every bit of the way.

Because God knows this: yes, he may have some specific stops in his will for us along the way, but we ultimately all have the same destination—heaven. And because of Jesus, nothing is going to stop us from getting there. His perfect will is to be with us forever. And that's going to happen—no matter what. So let God take you on adventures you never expected and lead you to places you never dreamed were even out there. And even if you get off track for a while, he'll always be willing to get you back to where you're supposed to be.

Life is not about standing still. It's about moving forward. Don't let "perfection" paralyze you. Get in the car and enjoy the ride, my friend.

You Have Freedom to Add to This List

I've had the joy of sharing the journeys of many women as they begin to move forward toward their God-sized dreams. One phrase I've found myself using over and over in that process is simply this: *you have freedom*. The response from my clients to that phrase is almost always the same word: "Really?"

So in case that question is still being whispered in your heart too, I want to answer: *yes, really.* It seems many of us (myself included) have struggled with feeling truly free to fully embrace what's already ours. It's as if we're still waiting for someone to tell us exactly what to do. But God has designed us to take responsibility for our lives. When we do, a whole lot of wonderful things start happening. We dream, take risks, and follow our purpose. We discover who we're created to be and begin to live it out. We mess up, make mistakes, and grow. Yes, those things can also be hard and scary too. And trying to be perfect can look easier in comparison. But it's not why God put us on this earth.

Jesus didn't die on the cross to make us perfect in God's eyes just so we could live our lives trying to make ourselves perfect too. When we do so, it's as if we're doubting what Jesus did is really enough. And you're not a doubter; you're a believer. Jesus died on the cross and was resurrected so that he could share life with you in this world and forever in heaven. When he said on the cross, "It is finished," he meant it.

What else do you need to add to what we've talked about in this list? Ask God to show you where you've let "perfectionism" get in the way of receiving the freedom that's already yours.

I've thought I had to be perfect by . . .

_____

_____

_____

But now I know I have freedom to . . .

_____

_____

_____

Embracing freedom doesn't mean running wild or demanding our rights. It simply means we accept what God has given us and move forward in faith. And if we mess up along the way, we make it right with God and keep going because we know we're loved no matter what. We all must come to a point where we truly answer this question: Is what Jesus did on the cross enough? If the answer to that question is yes, then we must stop adding to the gospel.

My visit with my parents eventually came to an end. I got up from my childhood bed, repacked my suitcase, and took one last look in the mirror. At the airport we hugged and promised to see each other again soon. I could see the mix of emotions in their eyes. They would miss me, and yet they also knew I was pursuing the life God had for me. Preparing me for that is why they gave me freedom as I grew up. And that's why they still accepted me in the times when that freedom led to mistakes. They could have chosen to keep me safe at all costs and controlled everything I did. But that's not what love does.

Freedom helps us become the person we're intended to be.

Perfectionism keeps us paralyzed by fear and stunts our growth.

God doesn't want to be a dictator who makes sure you simply do as you're told. Instead he wants you to take responsibility for your life and choose to obey him because of love.

You're not supposed to be perfect.

And you already have permission.

Every time you look into the mirror, tell the woman you see looking back at you that's true.

3

Trading Guilt for **Grace**

Perfectionism and guilt are best friends. Where you find one, you're likely to find the other. I had both as nearly constant companions in my childhood. Their presence showed itself as stomachaches and tension in my little body. Test after test at the doctor's office revealed nothing, because none of them could pinpoint the true trouble—my anxious heart.

It's a bit of a mystery to me why I struggled with feeling like I had to be perfect from such a young age. My parents weren't the put-on-the-pressure type. Perhaps some of us are just more naturally wired in ways that make us vulnerable to striving. I remember as a kid making goals like, "I'll ride around the block one hundred times" or "I'll swim one hundred laps" (yes, really, one hundred). No one told me to do this. And I never told anyone I did it. I enjoyed the challenge and felt an internal push to do more. That drive is one of my greatest strengths, but when I'm not watching it carefully, it's also the door through which guilt and perfectionism come sneaking into my life.

You may be rolling your eyes at my descriptions of being a mini-overachiever (I don't blame you—I think it annoyed the heck out of my little brother). But even if what I shared doesn't sound at all like you, it doesn't mean you didn't wrestle with the pressure to be perfect as a kid. Many of the women I've talked with dealt with perfectionism in completely different ways. Instead of "try harder" (my approach), they decided to handle the pressure by saying, "I won't try at all." Rather than pursuing challenges and chasing goals, they pulled back and stayed safe. Even when they wanted something, they didn't go for it, because doing so came with the risk of failure, and that was unacceptable.

Other women I've talked to decided "try harder" and "don't try at all" were both unappealing, and instead they'd deal with the pressure to be perfect with outright rebellion. Instead of riding their bikes around the block a hundred times, they were the ones smashing the mailboxes right along with the expectations everyone had for them. Their approach might be summed up not as "try harder" but instead "take that!" (Sometimes "try harder" types switch to this approach when they get really fed up—like I did when I headed off to college and rebelled.)

While our responses to the pressure to be perfect may be different, all of them have this in common: they eventually lead to guilt in one way or another. And dealing with that guilt is essential to our healing process.

I'm all grown up now, and while I've made a lot of progress, I still sometimes wrestle with feeling false guilt and as if I'm falling short. On the patio of a local coffee shop, I recently confessed that struggle to two dear friends. They had some words of wisdom for me. Words like, "You need to stop apologizing for who you are and the success God is creating in your life. It's time to quit feeling guilty." Right there on that patio, I pinky swore to both of them that I would change. This morning as I sat on my back porch and thought about this chapter, that conversation echoed in my ears and heart. How could I keep that promise? How could I learn to live without guilt? Because here's the shocking truth I'm learning to embrace: *God does not want us to feel guilty.*

How We Misunderstand Guilt

Guilt is not an emotional state in Scripture. It's a legal one. The first time we break God's law in even one small way, we are guilty. When we receive what Jesus did for us through his death and resurrection, we are no longer guilty. *Done.*

Yet even after God declares us "not guilty" through Jesus, we're still going to sin sometimes. So doesn't he want us to feel guilty again when that happens? Nope. Like we talked about before, guilt is a legal state in Scripture and not an emotional one. What God wants us to experience when we sin as believers is godly sorrow (sometimes called "conviction"), which is very different than what we would describe as "guilt."

The apostle Paul said, "Yet now I am happy, not because you were made sorry, but because your sorrow led you to repentance. For you became sorrowful as God intended and so were not harmed in any way by us" (2 Cor. 7:9). The word *sorry* comes from the word *sorrow*. It essentially says, "I feel grief over what I've done because it hurt someone I love." And here's the life-changing revelation: *guilt and sorrow are not the same thing.*

Guilt is self-focused.
Sorrow is grieving over how we've hurt someone else.

Guilt is a legal term.
Sorrow is a heart expression.

Guilt shuts us down.
Sorrow opens us up again.

Guilt leads to shame and distance.
Sorrow leads us to reconciliation and relationship.

Guilt simply discourages us.
Sorrow ultimately encourages us.

Guilt harms us.
Sorrow heals us.

Guilt holds us back.
Sorrow moves us toward what God has next.

We are to feel godly sorrow, but we can let go of guilt. Still, it's easy to let the latter slip back into our lives. Guilt often goes hand in hand with our personal attempts at perfection. When we fall short of what we think we *should* do, it's right there to point out our flaws and steal our joy.

If you're like me, a thought that may cross your mind is, "But I would be a total mess without guilt! It keeps me in line!" And that's exactly why we've got to get rid of the guilt, girl. We're not supposed to be pushed around by perfectionism and guilt. We're intended to be led by the Spirit and by love. Guilt is reinforcing your quest to make yourself perfect rather than receiving your identity from Jesus. And it's time to tell it good-bye.

Dear Guilt,

You and I have known each other for quite a while now. My whole life, really. We've been close at times. But most often our relationship has been challenging.

For one thing, you're unpredictable. You show up at parties unannounced. You wake me up in the middle of the night. You sit down by me at awkward times when I'm trying to have a conversation with someone I love.

And you're sneaky. You wear all sorts of disguises—humility, concern, even godliness. Just when I think I recognize you,

I find you get a new haircut, throw on a pair of shades, or dress up like someone else.

So here's what I'm saying: I think it's time for us to part ways. Because really, Guilt, we aren't doing each other a whole lot of good. You push me around. I enable you. It's not healthy.

I read this passage from a fabulous book called He Loves Me! *by Wayne Jacobsen. Here's what he had to say about getting rid of you:*

> *Until God disconnects you from the guilt and fear that drive your own performance, you will miss His love for you. How do you let guilt die? Endure it in his presence. I know that doesn't sound like much, but it will be enough. Stop doing what you do because you'll feel bad if you don't. When you feel guilt and condemnation roll over you like a late-afternoon thunderstorm, simply acknowledge that it is there and offer it to God.*[1]

My very wise friend also said this in an email to me when we were talking about you:

> *Guilt and shame are not tools that God uses to get us to do something he wants us to do, but they are instruments Satan uses to move us away from truth. I think because they mirror conviction (which is a good thing), we think they are of God and that he must be trying to tell us something. But guilt and shame do not match up with the character of God. Conviction does.*[2]

I think what she's saying is that you're an imposter. And I've got no time for that sort of thing in my life. I want the real deal—real love, real peace, real joy.

So, Guilt, this is good-bye. You may try to visit, but I'm letting you know the welcome mat is officially gone. And when you come you'll find your room is occupied by someone else who is much more loving, kind, and committed to my growth than you have ever been. Actually, I think I'll introduce you now—"Guilt, meet Grace."

*That should have happened a long time ago. It's really
been the Father's plan all along.*

Sincerely,

Holley

Sometimes we have trouble saying good-bye to guilt because
we don't recognize it in the first place. We think we're supposed
to feel bad. So we accept that as normal. I lived that way for a
long time, in part because I'm a good southern girl. And if there's
anything a good southern girl knows, it's this: everything goes
better with gravy. And guilt. Yes, a nice helping of guilt.

I feel guilty if I do too little. I feel guilty if I do too much. I even
feel guilty if I pause at a stoplight for two seconds after it turns
green. I imagine the people behind me glaring at the back of my
head for holding them up. Then I look in the mirror and there are
no cars behind me. *Yes, ma'am. That's how I roll.*

As I've recently looked more at what Scripture really says
about guilt, especially in the New Testament, here's what I've
discovered: guilt is always tied to a specific sin. Like we've
talked about before, it's a legal term. In other words, we have
clearly and intentionally broken a law. When we encounter that
kind of guilt, we confess our sin and ask forgiveness, then do
something different. Our guilt has already been taken care of
through Christ—we just need to receive what he's already done
on our behalf.

That kind of guilt is different than the gravy guilt many of us
experience.

Gravy guilt is poured over everything. It's not specific. It's
vague and hard to get a hold on.

Gravy guilt isn't about what I've done. It's about me. It tries
to cover who I really am and tell me I'm a no-good, pause-
at-the-light-too-long disgrace to southern society.

Gravy guilt also doesn't know about confession and forgiveness. It tells me that the only way to deal with it is to try harder. And when I've scraped every bit off my plate, another helping is already on the way.

So I think we all need to pause and ask ourselves, "Is this gravy guilt or God guilt (otherwise known as conviction or godly sorrow)?"

Conviction is temporary—it's a response to a specific sin and leads us to repentance.

Conviction never shames or condemns us—it calls us back to who we truly are.

Conviction is about a relationship—it helps us realize we've hurt Someone we love and prompts us to draw closer to him again.

What do you do when gravy guilt tries to cover the plate of your life? Same thing you probably learned to do at a dinner table somewhere. The hostess holds up that ladle, and you know you're about to get your potatoes drowned to oblivion. So you say, *"Oh, thank you, but I'm going to pass this time."* In other words, *"I'm not receiving that gravy guilt.* Not on my potatoes. Not on my heart. Not on my life." Then you make room on your plate for something really good. *A heaping helping of grace.* As much as you want. Seconds and thirds. Until you're all happy and full on the inside.

How Your Heart Can Respond to Grace

Once we say "no, thanks" to guilt and "yes, thanks" to grace, we still need a new response to replace our old heart habits. And that new response just may surprise you. I discovered it one day as a friend and I dug into our desserts with spoons in our hands and smiles on our faces. We caught up on our weeks in between comments that started with "Yum." I told her, "I'm still struggling with guilt. I feel like I've made progress, but it gets to me sometimes." Then I asked her, "What replaces guilt?" She answered with one simple word: *gratitude*. Huh. That's not what I expected. I was thinking more along the lines of my usual "try harder." But the more I pondered in the coming days and weeks, the more what she shared began making sense to me.

For example, let's say I go out to eat with my husband and feel guilty for spending the money (even though it's a special occasion and the meal fits our budget). That guilt keeps me from saying, "Thank you, God, for my husband. Thank you, God, for this delicious food and those who prepared it. Thank you, God, for the blessing of this amount that we can set aside for celebrations." Every time I make a list of all the things I feel guilty about, I discover each one offers ways to be grateful instead.

Not long after that conversation with my friend, I read a book that reinforced my new perspective. I finished it on a plane, and had our aircraft gone down, I think I would have clung to those pages as tightly as the oxygen mask dropping from the ceiling, because the truth in it made me feel like I could breathe again. I grew up in a denomination that leaned toward legalism. If you asked me about it, I would have said, "I dealt with all that years ago." And I did. On the outside. But on the inside, guilt and shame still had their way with me far too often, especially in moments of happiness and fun.

Author Gary Thomas challenged that with these words:

> Spiritual triumph begins and ends with finding our satisfaction in God above all things. We serve a generous God, however, who eagerly wants to bless us with many other pleasures, gifts from his hand that delight us—and in delighting us bring pleasure back to him. Rather than

seeing these gifts as competitors that steal our hearts from God, perhaps we can gratefully receive them and allow God to use them to ruin us to the ways of the world.

Prayer and fellowship are among life's richest pleasures, but let's not stop there. Let us learn to fill our souls with beauty, art, noble achievement, fine meals, rich relationships, and soul-cleansing laughter. When we acknowledge these pleasures, we acknowledge God as a genius creator of brilliant inventions. Let us be wary of a faith that denies these blessings as "worldly" and unfit, as though Satan rather than God had designed them. Let us refuse to fall into the enemy's trap of denying ourselves God's good pleasures so that we end up deeply vulnerable to illicit pleasure.[3]

You and I are made for joy. We are also made for happiness, fun, laughter, and enjoyment. We don't serve a taskmaster. We serve a good and faithful Father who finds delight in his children receiving his gifts. So let's open our hands, our hearts, and our lives a little wider to what he wants to freely give us today. *Then let's say thank you for it all.*

Next time you feel guilt trying to get the best of you, try responding with gratitude and praise instead. Here's a simple little process to help you do so.

· · · · · · · · · · · **When Guilt Tries to Get You** · · · · · · · · · ·

Ask yourself these questions:

○ What am I telling myself?

> *Example: I'm bad because the dust bunnies in my house are now the size of jackrabbits.*

○ What's the reality?

> *Yes, the house could use vacuuming. It's been a really busy week. I'll be able to do it next week.*

- What's the real truth? (This is a bridge statement between guilt/shame and gratitude/praise.)

  My worth is not based on the size of my dust bunnies. It's based on who Jesus says I am. And the reason my house is a bit dirty is because he's had other things for me to focus on over the last few days.

- What do I have to be grateful for and praise God about?

  God, thank you that I have a place to live. I praise you because you're my ultimate Home, and you're building me a mansion in heaven with no dust bunnies. Help me remember what matters most in light of eternity. Woo-hoo!

Now it's your turn to try it:

- What's a lie I've been telling myself?

  _____

  _____

- What's the reality?

  _____

  _____

- What's the real truth?

  _____

  _____

- What do I have to be grateful for and praise God about?

  _____

  _____

  _____

(Note: I've found that the "reality" and "truth" statements are essential. If I try to jump straight to gratitude and praise, then I bury the guilt and shame rather than healing it. We're human, and we need to acknowledge what we're feeling and experiencing before we can really change our perspective.)

Your body will help you know when it's time to ask yourself the questions above. I know I need to go through this process when I feel the muscles in my stomach tightening up, my heart beating harder, and my breathing becoming shallow. We respond physically when someone lies to us—and we do the same when we're lying to ourselves. How does your body tell you that something isn't quite right? Learn to be aware of that, and when you experience it, pause to take a deep breath, then go through the process above. If you get distracted along the way, that's okay. Just start again until you get all the way to the end.

Feelings of increasing anxiety also let us know guilt is trying to get us. When we start feeling anxious, it's a signal to pay attention to what we're telling ourselves so we can intentionally change those messages.

The great news is that changing our thought patterns really is possible. When we think the same thing over and over again, we create neural pathways in our minds, and those are associated with emotions. When we alter the way we think, we make new neural pathways and the old ones gradually fade away.

The process of true change takes time, practice, and patience. So if you don't "feel it" when you first try switching from guilt to gratitude (or any of the other new approaches we've talked about) that's totally normal. Just keep at it, and over time you can trust you will be "transformed by the renewing of your mind" (Rom. 12:2).

Switching from the Guilt Cycle to the Grace Cycle

The sooner we can identify guilt in our lives, the faster we can do something about it. So let's talk through a practical tool to help you: the Guilt Cycle and the Grace Cycle.

Imagine you open your eyes to a new day and a long list of to-dos. Before you're even out of bed, you notice a cobweb in the corner. Guilt creeps under the covers with you. You think of other women with cobweb-free corners (in their homes and hearts). You vow that today you'll try harder . . .

Can you relate to that pattern? If so, you're familiar with what I like to call the Guilt Cycle. It's like a little hamster wheel in our hearts that we run around again and again. It looks like this:

Guilt Cycle

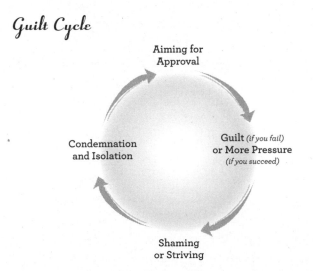

On another day you wake up and take a deep breath of grace. You believe you're loved and that whatever happens today, you will be okay. You slip into the kitchen with a smile for your first cup of coffee. You sit at the table with your to-do list and ask

God for his perspective on it. It seems like you can feel him with you as you check off the first item. Of course, the day doesn't go as planned. And you even mess up a few times. But you go to bed knowing that you're cherished just as much as when the day started.

Can you relate to that pattern? If so, you're familiar with what I like to call the Grace Cycle. Instead of a hamster wheel, it's a safe space for our hearts to rest and thrive.

Grace Cycle

Receiving
Grace

Freedom
and Joy

Love and
Intimacy

Obedience
and Service

If you're living like I did for many years, the Guilt Cycle sneaks up on you and you step into it without even realizing you've done so until you're exhausted. Thankfully, God wants to help us go through our days differently. To trade guilt for grace. How can that actually happen? Here's a start . . .

Getting from the Guilt Cycle to the Grace Cycle

- Listen for the lie. What are you telling yourself that isn't true? For example, "I'm not doing enough."
- Replace the lie with grace-filled truth. For example, "I can do all things through Christ who strengthens me. But he never asks me to do it all!"

- Ask God for help. Whisper a prayer saying, "I'm on the hamster wheel of the Guilt Cycle again. I want to step off of it and back into grace. Please forgive me and help me receive what I need from you right now."
- Call for backup if needed. In the times when you can't remember what's true and even saying a prayer feels like too much, reach out to someone you trust and let them help you off the unmerry-go-round of the Guilt Cycle.
- Do it again tomorrow . . . or two minutes from now.

Pause for a moment and ask yourself: Which cycle am I in at this moment? If you're in the Guilt Cycle, how can you switch to the Grace Cycle based on what we've just talked through together? If you're in the Grace Cycle, what's one thing that's helping you be there today?

_____

_____

_____

Staying Guilt-Free for Life

When patterns have been part of who we are for years, we often need help changing them. Seek out grace-giving people to share this journey with you. They will be able to keep speaking truth to you when perfectionism tries to call your name again.

I recently picked up my phone in the middle of a wild week to text a friend about a lie that my heart kept hearing. Then I simply asked, "What's the truth? I can't come up with it right now." She wrote back and told me what I already knew deep inside but couldn't quite recall in the moment. I sat and read her words over and over, then got up with new strength to face the day.

Years ago I wouldn't have sent that text. I would have tried to come up with the truth on my own. I would have given in to shame and guilt. I would have spent the day thinking about how everyone else was more spiritual than me and how I should try harder. But I'm learning this: it really is okay to call for backup.

Most of us know the story of the man lowered down through a roof by his friends so he could be laid at the feet of Jesus and find healing (see Mark 2:1–12). We all have days when our hearts, not our bodies, need the same thing. We think if we can just muster up enough "faith," then we should be able to get there ourselves. But that's not the way it works. And, friend, when we refuse to let others help us, it's not being spiritual ... it's pride. (Yeah, I don't like hearing that either.)

We're made to share life with each other. We're made to say, "I need you. Please help me." Those aren't words of weakness—they're the strongest words we can say. It's easy to try to figure things out on our own. It's much harder to say, "Please carry my heart to Jesus today." But you know what? The man who was healed that day wasn't the only one who received a blessing. His friends did too because they got to be part of the work God was doing. Give people in your life that same opportunity.

The pinky swear promise I made to stop living in guilt has been harder to keep than it felt like it would be in that sun-soaked moment with friends on the coffee shop patio. Because it's in the dark and quiet when no one is around that guilt and perfection come knocking. Sometimes I remember what's true, and at other times I seem to completely forget. And that's okay. God doesn't ask us to get over our struggles all at once. He only asks us to be committed to "growing in the grace" of Jesus (see 2 Pet. 3:18). That's something we can all do because it's about believing and receiving, not trying harder.

Pinky promise with me you'll learn to live with less guilt too?

It's time, friend.

And I'm praying right now for your heart to soon be set free in new ways.

Stop Apologizing for Who You Are

Stop trying to downplay your gifts.

Stop trying to minimize your successes.

Stop trying to skim over your strengths with, "Oh, that was nothing."

It was not nothing.

It was the spark of God within you.

It was who he created you to be, shining bright.

It was what he called you to, coming forth into the world.

Don't listen to the whiners, the discouragers, the critics, the good-in-your-life-makes-me-feel-bad crowd.

You have nothing to be sorry for, sister.

Those things aren't a reason for an apology—they're reasons for gratitude, celebration, and praise.

Hold your head high. Keep that joy in your heart. Let your light shine.

It's the proper response to what God has done (and is doing) through you.

And if anyone tells you to tone it down—they can take it up with him.

4

What Your Heart Really Needs Is **Perfect Love**

Even when we desperately want to be free, one thing often keeps our hearts in bondage: *fear*.

Fear that we won't be enough.
Fear that we will be rejected.
Most of all, fear that we won't be loved.

That's why simply telling ourselves, "I'm going to stop trying to be perfect," never quite works. We resolve to strive less and relax more, but in the end we fall back into old patterns. We long for something new to grow in the place of our fears. Thankfully, God has promised just what our hearts need: *perfect love*. "There is no fear in love. But perfect love drives out fear, because fear has to do with punishment" (1 John 4:18).

Perfect love can be hard to understand and embrace because we don't experience it from each other this side of heaven. Even those closest to us can hurt us or let us down sometimes. When we understand the different ways God perfectly loves us like no human can, our hearts can finally be healed and free.

God Loves You Like a Perfect Father

She sits in my counseling office and slowly shreds a tissue into a hundred little pieces. As I watch her, I imagine that's how her heart must feel too. With head lowered, she tells of a father who wounded with words and hands. It only took the slightest mistake. A cup knocked over at dinner. A report card with one B. A laugh that was a little too loud.

She's learned to be a pleaser to keep the peace. And that choice has brought its rewards. She's climbing the corporate ladder, but each rung only brings with it the knowledge that now she has farther to fall. She lives looking over her shoulder, waiting for someone to tell her that she's going to be punished. She admits, "It's so hard for me to believe God loves me when so much of my life has been shaped by a demanding parent and now is driven by my performance." She tears off the last corner of the tissue and looks up with determination. "But I'm tired," she says. "I don't want to live this way anymore." I lean forward and smile, and we get started on seeing God in a whole new way.

Our earthly fathers are the first influence on how we relate to God. Even the very best and most loving dads are still human, and none of them can fully show us who God is. We all have work to do when it comes to changing our perspective of our heavenly Father. We're not going to analyze what your dad did or didn't do. There can be a time and place for that, but it's not here. Instead I think what matters most is that we see how God *does* perfectly love us. When we do so, the false perceptions we've picked up from our earthly fathers will quickly become obvious.

Abuse is so painful because it's the complete opposite of what God intends us to receive from our fathers. *God will never, ever harm you.* Yes, because you live in a broken world, there will be hurt in your life sometimes, but there's a very big difference between *hurt* and *harm.* Dr. Henry Cloud explains it this way: "Surgery hurts: it is good for us. It hurts but it does not injure or harm us. . . . Hurt does not mean harm. Harm is when we injure people by doing destructive things to them."[1]

When fathers speak or act in destructive ways toward their children, we learn to equate hurt with harm. This is especially true with punishment. *God disciplines us, but he does not punish us.* "Fear has to do with punishment. The one who fears is not made perfect in love" (1 John 4:18).

Punishment comes from anger.
Discipline comes from love.

Punishment is someone coming down on us.
Discipline is someone seeking to lift us up.

Punishment wounds our hearts.
Discipline keeps us from greater hurt.

Punishment makes us feel bad about who we are.
Discipline affirms our identity as beloved daughters.

Proverbs 3:12 says, "The LORD disciplines those he loves, as a father the son he delights in." For us as women it would read, "The LORD disciplines those he loves, as a father the daughter he delights in." If the way you were punished—whether with words, physical acts, or other methods—did not make you feel like a daughter who was delighted in, then your parent was not accurately reflecting your heavenly Father. That doesn't mean your parent didn't love you. They may even have been trying their best. But it does mean there's an incorrect perception of God in your heart that needs to be changed.

A Loving Father Protects You

Not only does God not punish us, he wants to protect us. So many women view God as the one coming after them rather than the one rescuing them. We will never know this side of heaven how many times God has actually intervened on our behalf, but we can trust that he does. My husband and I recently discovered the television series *24*. In the show, Kiefer Sutherland plays agent Jack Bauer. In the first season, Jack goes through more than most of us can imagine in a lifetime with the goal of simply doing this: getting his daughter back. I don't watch that show and think, "No father would ever do that. She isn't worth it. Just let her go." No, the show is so compelling because we instinctively know fathers are supposed to protect their daughters—even if it costs their own lives. And when Jesus died on the cross for you, it did.

You may wonder, "Then why do bad things happen to us?" Because we live in a fallen, broken world full of fallen, broken people. Even in this unsafe world, God does promise our *security*. God is fighting for us, and one day he'll come for us. Whatever we go through in this life will not last forever. One day we'll have a new home where no harm will ever come to us again.

A Loving Father Gives You What's Best

Your heavenly Father's desire is not only to protect you but also to provide for your needs. You may have asked your earthly father for love and gotten rejection instead. You may have sought approval and instead been answered with criticism. You may have wanted to be seen as beautiful and instead encountered abuse. Experiences like that create within us a fear of what God might give us. But Jesus says, "Which of you, if your son asks for bread, will give him a stone? Or if he asks for a fish, will give him a snake? If you, then, though you are evil, know how to give good gifts to your children, how much more will your Father in heaven give good gifts to those who ask him!" (Matt. 7:9–11).

The examples Jesus gives are especially beautiful because the father is giving directly to the child, which requires attention and engagement. Even if your dad didn't abuse you, you may have simply felt overlooked. Maybe your father worked a lot of overtime. Maybe he had a hobby that stole his heart and extra hours. Maybe it felt like his eyes were always on the television instead of you. If so, God wants to whisper this to you: "My daughter, you are worthy of attention."

God is fully engaged in every detail of what happens with you. "Even the very hairs on your head are all numbered" (Matt. 10:30). He is never too tired, busy, or distracted to pay attention to you. Sometimes we think if we're perfect daughters, then our dads will finally truly notice us. They'll come home from work early, turn off the TV, or spend more time with us on the weekends. But those actions by our fathers are not about us—and they never have been. Our dads are broken people too, and we need to give them grace, then turn to God to receive what our earthly fathers simply can't offer.

A Loving Father Is There for You

Maybe you're thinking it would be nice to even *have* a dad. Yours might have left before you were born or somewhere along the way. So you have a dad-shaped hole inside you just crying out for someone to fill it. That makes you vulnerable to trying to be perfect for the father figures in your life so they will approve of you and ease that ache. But God is the only one who can meet the need any of us have for a father—whether we physically have one in our lives or not.

All of us can ask God to give us what our heart needs from a father and know that he will respond in love. You might start by simply asking him this: "God, will you please replace all my false perceptions of you as my heavenly Father with what's really true?" He will not punish, harm, or deny you what is best. He will not tell you to come back later. He will not dismiss your needs or criticize your hopes. You are secure with God forever.

You are a beloved daughter with a Father who perfectly loves you.

What's one way God has loved you like a Father?

_____

_____

God Loves You Like the Perfect Friend

In high school the little youth group I attended was my whole social world. One girl and I grew particularly close. Then suddenly I began feeling distance between us. I wrote her a letter telling her I was sorry if I'd done anything to hurt her and that I still cared about her. I never heard back, and she didn't talk to me at church anymore. Another one of her friends told me, "She got your note and she made fun of it." And a small piece of my heart began to hide, because I didn't know what I'd done, but I did know this: some part of me was not good enough, and I must try harder.

We first learn love at home. But then we go out into the world and our peers influence how we feel about who we are. We find out there's a certain way we're supposed to dress, talk, and act and even particular items that belong in our lunch boxes. We skin our knees on the sidewalk, and we skin our hearts in conversations. We carry those scars, and we promise ourselves we'll do whatever it takes to never feel that away again. Even if it means being perfect.

Soon our friendships aren't about growing connections but rather avoiding rejection. We hide who we are and try to fit in. Our souls start feeling cramped and we long for a way out, a place where we can breathe a bit easier. But fear keeps us confined within walls of our own making. We find out that "perfect" is a lonely place to be, because even when you're with people you're not fully there.

Even when we find a friend who is true to us, they'll eventually disappoint us or let us down in some way. And we'll do the same—not because we want to but because we're human. We work through it, forgive, reconnect, but there's still a longing in our hearts for the perfect friend. That's what Jesus offers to be to us. He says, "I have called you friends" (John 15:15) and "Greater love has no one than this: to lay down one's life for one's friends" (John 15:13).

Of all the ways God addresses us, "friends" seems the most scandalous to me. Because we *choose* our friends. We spend time with them because we *want* to. We willingly open our hearts and lives to them. And yet it's in that place of friendship where many of us need the most healing. When God says he's our "friend," it can feel unsafe because friends haven't treated us well. What does it really mean to have a friend?

A Loving Friend Chooses You

We are born into families, but we pick our friendships. When God says you're his friend, he's saying *he wants you*. For many years I thought what God felt toward me was obligation. He had to love me. He had to put up with me. But when he calls us "friends," it changes everything.

A Loving Friend Enjoys You

We spend time with friends for many different reasons, but one clearly is this: we like to be together. Studies have shown that being with friends is one of life's most enjoyable activities. We love our friends, but we also really like them too. When God says you're his friend, it means he likes you too. He enjoys you. He wants to be with you. "The LORD delights in those who fear him, who put their hope in his unfailing love" (Ps. 147:11).

A Loving Friend Doesn't Speak Negatively about You

Most of the wounds in friendships come from words. Someone makes a critical remark about us, we overhear a bit of gossip, or we feel judged rather than accepted when we need it most. We can picture God the same way. We imagine him in heaven listing off our faults or the ways we could do better. But it's the devil who is the accuser of our brothers and sisters (see Rev. 12:10). That negative, critical, condemning voice in your mind, heart, or life is not God.

One source of this false belief is how we picture what will happen when we die and go before God for judgment. We imagine we'll hear all we've done wrong. But listen to how 1 Corinthians 4:5 describes that scene instead: "He will bring to light what is hidden in darkness and will expose the motives of the heart. *At that time each will receive their praise from God*" (emphasis added). Did you catch that? We will receive *praise* from God. Not criticism. Not accusation. Not condemnation. Because of Jesus, we will receive praise. God will talk to us like a friend.

A Loving Friend Is Your Advocate and Encourager

Not only does Jesus not speak negatively about you, but he is actually your advocate. He defends you when the enemy tries to speak against you. "If anybody does sin, we have an advocate with the Father—Jesus Christ, the Righteous One" (1 John 2:1). The enemy is the accuser; Jesus is the advocate. And the Holy Spirit speaks encouragement into our lives, reminding us of who we truly are and what we're called to do. One reason we strive so hard to be perfect is to silence that critical voice in our minds. So let's pause right now and agree on this together: *that critical voice is not God.* However it came into your life, the real source is the enemy of your soul. God is not your enemy. He is your friend. And friends love each other with their words.

A Loving Friend Speaks the Truth to You with Grace

You know someone cares about you when they're willing to say, "Hey, you've got some spinach in your teeth." And as a good friend, God does the same with us. His Spirit tells us when we need to remove something from our lives. When he does so, it's always about the sin and not about who we are. The enemy will say, "You're a failure." God will say, "You've fallen down. You don't belong there. Let me help you back up."

A Loving Friend Helps You Become All You're Created to Be

The true test of friendship is this: Does this person want me to be who I am or turn me into someone else? God created you for a purpose. He knit you together in your mother's womb. He gave you strengths, skills, and a unique design. He doesn't want you to change who you are; he wants you to become *more* of who you are. Beware of anyone who says, "To please God, you must be like me (or us)." No, Jesus has already made you pleasing to God through his death on the cross and his resurrection. Now he wants you to be you. And God loves variety. Think about your friends and how there's something different you love about each one of them. Would you want them all to be the same? Nope. And God feels the same way about his friends too.

So how do we help our hearts heal from the wounds we've experienced in friendship so that we can stop trying to be perfect to protect ourselves? Ironically, it starts with us choosing to be the kind of friend we want to have. As long as we are hurting our sisters, we will not be able to receive the healing God has for us as his friends. And we usually have to make the first move.

My dear friend Ann Voskamp shares this about an encounter with a friend:

> We share a no-fat sticky bun together on a Monday morning with a glass of orange juice and we don't believe for a New York minute that that sticky sweet won't find our hips. We laugh. I meet her friends. They are wondrous. My mouth feels dry. She drives me to the airport.
>
> And when I am back home on the farm, she writes me a letter, and I keep it.
>
>> You have been hurt by women. I could see the pain in your eyes ... And I've never done this before but ... I feel prompted to make you a promise of friendship.
>>
>> *I promise I will never speak an unkind word to or about you. I will never be jealous of you. I will never compete with you. I will never abandon or betray you. I will love you. I will pray for you. I will do all I can to help you go far and wide in the Kingdom.*
>>
>> *I will accept you as you are, always. I will be loyal to you. Before our loving God of grace, you have my words and my heart in friendship for this life and forever with him.*

And our God is a love body and he hates amputations and he sutures our wounds together with the silver threads of community. And I have found healing in this community of women.

In this place, we kneel down beside you. In this place, we reach out our hands. In this place, can you hear us whisper?

"You have been hurt. We can see the pain in your eyes—We offer you a promise of friendship."

In the places of sisters and sinners and souls made saints, we make safe circles around women and together we watch each other's backs and together we bend down when one hunches over in pain.

And together we pick up the shards of the hearts all shattered, the Jesus-women making this healing mosaic of grace.[2]

I'm the girl who wrote Ann that letter. When I did, I thought of my friend all those years ago back in youth group who hurt me and how I never wanted any of my sisters to go through the same. And when I promised Ann she was safe with me, I knew in a new way that I was safe with Jesus. That he truly was my friend. That what happened to Ann and I at the hands of women had hurt him too. It's a mystery, but I wholeheartedly believe one of the best ways to get free from our own pursuit of perfection is to offer grace and safety to others. Because as we love like Jesus, we understand more of how he offers the same to us too.

You are a friend of God, and he not only loves you—he really likes you too.

What's one way God has loved you like a friend?

_____

_____

God Loves You Like a Perfect Husband

The prince falls in loves with Cinderella. He searches the kingdom for her and slides the glass slipper on her foot like an engagement ring. We all know how the story ends: "And they lived happily ever after." We also know that's not how real-life stories usually go. Fast-forward a year later and the prince is upset because Cinderella has spent too much money on this season's glass slippers at her favorite store. And she's locked herself in her bedroom to cry into her pillow about the unemotional man she married.

We go into marriage with a lot of expectations. And even if we marry someone wonderful, those expectations aren't going to be met. I watched a documentary last night called *This Emotional Life*. One segment followed a couple through their whirlwind romance, the birth of four children, an affair, several sessions of couples therapy, and their eventual reconciliation. The therapist said something like, "I have a lot of hope for them because they really do love and respect each other." Even with all the mess and misunderstanding, he believed they could make it. Love is a powerful thing. And even when it's incredibly hard, we want to believe in it. We all want the fairy tale—the happily ever after with a perfect husband.

And here's the thing: there's nothing wrong with that desire. It's just that we misplace it sometimes. Yes, you have a perfect husband. His name is Jesus, and one day you'll be in heaven with him for your happily-ever-after story. But it's easy to forget that and instead insist that the men in our lives fulfill those needs. For those us of who are married, we look to our flesh-and-blood husbands, and for those of us who are single, we look to the yet-to-marry-him men of our fantasies.

In *So Long, Insecurity* Beth Moore says, "Men are not our problem; it's what we are trying to get from them that messes us up. Nothing is more baffling than our attempt to derive our womanhood from our men. We use guys like mirrors to see if we're valuable. Beautiful. Desirable. Worthy of notice. Viable."[3] When those mirrors don't reflect what we hope to see, our usual response is *try harder*. Maybe we buy a new outfit. Spend a few more minutes on our makeup. Try to cook better dinners. Keep the house tidier. Be a bit more enthusiastic about football. Some part of us believes, "If I'm the perfect wife, then he has to love me and stay with me forever."

But as too many women know, it often doesn't work out that way. And we end up blaming ourselves for the unraveling of our relationships, which only makes us work harder to be sure that never happens again. *Your heart is not created for that kind of striving.* It wounds you as a woman and your husband as a man. No human relationship can completely fulfill your need for love. When the men we love fall short, it's a signal to our souls to turn to Jesus instead. But we often think of Jesus as not being pleased with us either.

But over and over, when Scripture describes us as a bride, it is with joyful words like these: "As a young man marries a young woman, so will your Builder marry you; as a bridegroom rejoices over his bride, so will your God rejoice over you" (Isa. 62:5). In Song of Songs, which many scholars see as a being about Jesus and his bride, the groom says, "You are altogether beautiful, my darling; there is no flaw in you" (4:7). Even at the end of Proverbs 31 where the ideal woman is described, the chapter closes with these affirming words:

> Her husband . . . praises her:
> "Many women do noble things,
>   but you surpass them all."
> Charm is deceptive, and beauty is fleeting;
>   but a woman who fears the LORD is to be
>   praised.

> Honor her for all that her hands have done,
> and let her works bring her praise at the
> city gate. (Prov. 31:28–30)

There's simply no escaping this theme in Scripture: Jesus delights in his bride. Yes, we can break his heart just like an adulterous wife can break her husband's. But overall, when we love Jesus and are faithful to him, the response from his heart is *joy*.

A Loving Husband . . .

- is patient with his wife
- shows her kindness
- rejoices in her successes and blessings
- doesn't try to seem "better" than her
- approaches her with humility
- honors her
- puts her needs above his own

- doesn't easily get angry with her
- forgives fully and freely
- reminds her of what is true
- protects her
- trusts her
- helps her have hope for the future
- never, ever gives up on her

(based on 1 Cor. 13)

If you're thinking, "My husband doesn't do everything on that list," then that's exactly the point. *No husband does*. And as long as you keep expecting a man to love you like only Jesus can, you will keep trying to earn that love by being perfect.

Here's what your heart needs to hear:

You don't have to be the perfect wife on this earth.

You will be the perfect wife of the perfect husband in heaven forever.

I'll admit how all that works is a mystery to me. But whatever that looks like exactly, I do know this: the longing we feel for love as women will be completely fulfilled in heaven by Christ.

You don't have to try harder. You've just got to wait a bit longer. There's a big difference between those two. And in the meantime, you can rest in knowing you're loved beyond what you can even imagine right now.

You are a beautiful bride loved by a perfect husband.

What's one way God has loved you like a husband?

_____

_____

Note: Because Jesus loves you, he doesn't want to see you abused in any way. Knowing we will not have a perfect husband in this lifetime doesn't mean we should put up with anything and everything in our marriages. If you're experiencing harm from your husband, see a professional counselor and make sure you're safe.

God Loves You Like a Perfect Leader

Janet leans on her desk and buries her face in her hands. Her elbows rest on a new stack of reports her boss has demanded she complete by the end of the day. She knows it's impossible, but it doesn't matter—she'll get a lecture anyway.

Amy sits in the church pew on Sunday, and the words coming from the pulpit feel as hard as the wood beneath her. She glances at the other women around her diligently taking notes and sighs. "Get it together, Amy," she says to herself. "This person is your spiritual leader."

Sarah misses an easy two-point shot on the basketball court. She can hear her coach's footsteps approaching and then a voice in her ear. "What's the matter with you? I knew I should never have let you on the team. You're letting everyone down."

Leaders influence us in powerful ways. Teachers, coaches, pastors, bosses—they all shape how we see ourselves and the standards we believe we need to meet in order to be acceptable. They can hand out gold stars or snuff out the light in our souls. When leaders are harsh or demanding, it's easy to view God the same way. We begin picturing him as never being satisfied with our performance. No matter how hard we work, it's not enough. We get tired. We think we have to be perfect. We might even give up. But God wants us to show us instead how we're really supposed to be loved by leaders.

Loving Leaders Give People Freedom to Fail

I recently attended a multiday innovation training session by the leadership team at the Eureka! Ranch. One phrase they used over and over again was "Fail fast, fail cheap." They encouraged us to make mistakes, make them quickly, and make them often. They challenged the group to applaud unsuccessful attempts because they are part of the learning process and contribute to eventual success. Someone had an idea that didn't end up working, and we actually cheered. It was a little mind-blowing.

Whether in corporate America or church pews on Sunday morning, we don't like to talk about mistakes. But God isn't so shy about it. He knows we're human, and when we mess up it's not a surprise to him. When we make a mistake, it's a natural part of the growth process. We fall a lot when we're learning to walk, and that doesn't stop when we're grown-ups. When a leader doesn't give his or her followers freedom to fail, growth is stunted. The authors of *Toxic Faith* say:

> The rule of perfectionism denies the follower the right to embrace the limits of the human condition. If the individual has never dealt with feelings of inadequacy and inferiority and never accepted individual limits, each mistake will seem devastating. The victim will be driven to perform, measure up, and do things "right" to avoid feelings of inadequacy and insecurity. The practice of faith becomes obsessed with performance.[4]

When we start performing rather than growing, what's best in us gets buried. We hide our gifts, hold back our strengths, and avoid opportunities that stretch us. We feel safer, but we're slowly dying inside.

The best leaders say, "Go ahead and try. If you mess up, we will work through it together." They're gentle with those who fail, and they never withhold their love. Even after Peter denied Jesus three times on the night before the crucifixion, Jesus restored their relationship and reinstated Peter as a disciple.

Any leader who demands absolute perfection and doesn't allow you to ever be human is not reflecting the heart of God toward his people.

Loving Leaders Serve Those in Their Care

People seek leadership for many different reasons. Some want the power. Others seek the recognition and status. Many desire control and to push forward an agenda. Very few say, "I want to be a leader so I can serve." Even when politicians and other public figures make such statements, their actions often don't align with their words.

A candidate promises to serve those who helped elect him and is then caught dipping his hands into campaign funds.

A preacher commits to staying with his congregation for a certain amount of time and then suddenly runs away to a fancier, better-paying church with no explanation.

A CEO says she'll turn the company around and then hires all her friends for the executive team while dismissing those who have been there for decades.

Leaders are human, and while their selfishness may not be as obvious as the examples above, many simply don't lead with the best interest of the people under their care in mind. God had harsh words for religious leaders who treated his people this way: "Therefore this is what the LORD, the God of Israel, says to the shepherds who tend my people: 'Because you have scattered my flock and driven them away and have not bestowed care on them, I will bestow punishment on you for the evil you have done,' declares the LORD" (Jer. 23:2). Then he promises, "I will place shepherds over them who will tend them, and they will no longer be afraid or terrified, nor will any be missing" (Jer. 23:4).

If a leader over you does not care for you or is using fear to manipulate you, then that person had better watch out. They're abusing a position God has allowed them to be in, and they're accountable to him for their actions toward others. You are to love that person and fulfill your duties with excellence, but you are not obligated to please every authority figure. Jesus, your Shepherd, serves those in his care and was even willing to lay down his life for you. That is what faithful leaders do.

Loving Leaders Help People Become Who They Are

The biggest red flag to look for when it comes to a leader or organization is this: Do they pressure you to conform to *who they are*, or do they help you become more of *who you are*? Leaders who want people to be perfect usually have very specific definitions of what that word means.

Perfect people work on weekends.
Perfect people volunteer for every committee.
Perfect people dress, talk, and act a certain way.

In other words, *perfect people do whatever makes the leader look good.*

God is not that kind of leader. He created us with remarkable individuality, and he expresses himself through us in highly unique ways. Ephesians 2:10 says we are "God's masterpiece"

(NLT). Author Emily P. Freeman explains more about what that really means:

> Those English words used in the text—*masterpiece*, sometimes translated *workmanship*—these are translations of the original word used in the letter to the church at Ephesus, the Greek word *poiema*. Our English word *poem* comes from this same Greek word. Workmanship, masterpiece, poem—all these words in Scripture are used to describe God's work—you and me.[5]

God sees you not as project but as a poem. He does not want you to conform to certain standards but instead to be an expression of who he is in this world. *If a leader demands that you meet excessive, unrealistic expectations, then that person is trying to put you back under the law.* Early Christians in the Galatian church dealt with this dilemma, and Paul told them, "It is for freedom that Christ has set us free. Stand firm, then, and do not let yourselves be burdened again by a yoke of slavery" (Gal. 5:1). In other words, don't let anyone be your master except Christ, and always remember that he is a master who gives freedom. What is the goal of that freedom? Love. Obedience that flows from a relationship. You becoming who God created you to be.

You are allowed to respectfully question your leaders. Even God said, "Come now, let us reason together" (Isa. 1:18 ESV). Be careful of any authority who is not open to differences or discussions. If someone is completely closed off to input from others, then take it as a major sign that it may be time to get out from under that person's leadership.

God gives us the freedom to bring our thoughts, feelings, and questions to him because he doesn't just want your performance—he wants much more than that. *He wants you as a person.* And not so he can strip away your individuality but so he can express himself through it. Trying to be perfect always makes us less of who we are.

You are under the care of a perfect leader who loves you.

What's one way God has loved you like a leader?

_____

_____

People will never love us perfectly. And when they don't, it's easy to assume it's our fault. We tell ourselves, "I'll try harder to be perfect so I can be loved." But that's a treadmill that will lead us nowhere except to burnout and frustration.

Yes, we do need perfect love. But we can only get it from one place: God's heart. If we see him as demanding, demeaning, or simply apathetic, then we'll keep running toward other sources. Every quest for perfection has at its root some incorrect belief about how God loves us. We pick up those lies from all kinds of places without even realizing it. Ask God to show you where you've accidentally accepted what isn't true and replace it with what your heart really needs instead. You don't have to live in fear anymore. Instead you can believe by faith . . .

God is for you.

God is with you.

God loves you beyond all you can even imagine.

Right here. Right now. *As you are.*

The God Who **Loves You** More Than You Know

Imagine you walk to your mailbox and find three letters with loving words inside. One is from an anonymous sender. Another is from a friend. The third is from someone you know intimately. Which person's words would mean the most to you? I'm guessing the third. The more we know the one who loves us, the more that person's love means to us. So let's take some time to learn more about who God is—the God who loves you, who hung the stars in place, who numbers every hair on your head and knows every care in your heart.

Sometimes God's love seems especially real. I experienced that once as a South Carolina sky spread above me. It was freckled with stars in the still-dark of early morning. I looked from east to west and tried to find the end of the universe. But it just went on and on. I thought of these words: "For as high as the heavens are above the earth, so great is his love for those who fear him; as far as the east is from the west, so far has he removed our transgressions from us" (Ps. 103:11–12).

In those quiet moments on a front porch before dawn, I felt small and God seemed infinitely big. I'd shared a weekend with fellow writers in a beach house, and now I was heading to the airport. We'd talked about our dreams, struggles, hopes, and fears. All of those were given new perspective as I stared at the sky.

Yes, we need to understand who we are and how much we're loved. But we can't stop there—what really sets us free from perfectionism is remembering who God is. Because when we see the distance between our humanity and his divinity, it quickly becomes clear that achieving perfection is impossible for us. It would be like me thinking I could reach up to grab one of those stars and tuck it in my pocket.

I come to this chapter with a bit of trembling, because who am I to talk about who God is? I've walked with him most of my life. And yet I understand that trying to fully understand him is like trying to fit the ocean in a thimble. He's beyond our comprehension, beyond all we can imagine, more than our human hearts can even understand. Yet he's also near and calls us his friends. He's a paradox and a glorious mystery. So I will do my best to offer what I can in words about someone I love.

God Is Love

Love is where we must always begin with God. "Whoever does not love does not know God, because God is love" (1 John 4:8). Through the years I've looked into the eyes of hurting women and asked, "Do you really believe God loves you—not just tolerates you?" Most often the reaction is tears springing to their eyes. Somehow we've gotten the idea that God simply "puts up with us" because he has to. We're the naughty children who drive him crazy, but he has to be our parent anyway. I believe *at the root of every human quest for perfection is a misunderstanding of God's love for us.* Our hearts are made for love, and if we don't think we can freely receive it, then we'll try to earn it.

God doesn't just love you; he *is* love. It's the essence of his character. *God can't be unloving.* It's simply not possible. And his love is far different than what we've experienced from other people.

God's love has no limits. You can't wear him out or be too much for him to handle. He doesn't grow tired. He doesn't have bad days. His response to you doesn't depend on his mood or energy level. There's never an end to his love for you.

God's love has no expectations. In every human relationship, we encounter expectations. But God doesn't have any for us. He already knows our hearts, and therefore we can't surprise or disappoint him.

God's love has no requirements. We're used to relationships in which we're made to feel, "If you do X, then I will love you." God's love is unconditional. God loved all of us while we were still sinners, and nothing can separate us from his love now.

God's love is not dependent on us. Human love is often determined by our actions. But God loves us because that's who he is. It's part of his character. He will always love us, no matter what we do.

God's love has our ultimate good in mind. Because he doesn't need our love, God can do what is best for us even if it's not what we want. Other people may make choices that aren't really beneficial to us just so we won't get upset with them. But God is independent of us and doesn't need our approval.

God's love can't be earned. It can only be received. We can win the affections of others through our actions. But God's love is only and always a gift of grace. We can never be good enough to gain his love and never bad enough to lose it.

It's hard to wrap our minds around this kind of love because it's so different than human love. In *He Loves Me! Learning to Live in the Father's Affection*, author Wayne Jacobsen says:

> Two thousand years of religious tradition have inculcated in us the mistaken notion that God's love is something we earn. If we do what pleases him, he loves us; if not, he doesn't. Giving that up isn't easy. Moving from a performance-based religious ethic to a relationship deeply rooted in the Father's affection is no small transition.[1]

But it's a transition we have to make if we're ever going to beat perfectionism, because God's love is the only thing that can truly defeat it.

When we look at God's love, it should feel like looking at the stars—an act that puts who we are and all our efforts back into perspective. God's love is bigger and vaster than we can even fathom. It can't ever be fully understood, only gratefully received. And it certainly can't be possessed through our actions. Either God's love is real and what Jesus did on the cross is enough, or we're all doomed. There is no in-between. Trying to be perfect is an illusion as surely as thinking I can jump to the moon. Decide once and for all: Is God's love real or not? We can live a lifetime saying we believe it is and living like it's not. Grace and law can't coexist. It's either one or the other.

God is offering his love to you—fully, freely, and forever.

God Is Holy

The word *love* in our culture is often watered down to a "do whatever makes you feel good" emotion. So when I tell people God is love, the response I often get is, "But he's not *just* love. He's also holy." In other words, he's not the spoil-the-child parent who lets little Susie get away with whatever she wants while standing by and smiling. And yes, that's absolutely true. But misunderstanding God's holiness can push us to the opposite extreme of seeing God only as a strict disciplinarian who wants to make sure his kids toe the line and make him look good. So let's talk about what it really means when God tells us he's holy and that we are to be too.

The word *holy* essentially means *different*. And God is different from us in every way. He asks us to be different from the world around us too. We are set apart as his people. When we hear this we can instantly say, "Okay, I will make a holiness checklist. I will do this, this, and that. And I will never do that, that, or this." With sincere hearts, we set out to please God, and without even meaning to, we can end up as Pharisees.

That's because the process of holiness is never meant to be in our hands. "By one sacrifice he has made perfect forever those who are *being made holy*" (Heb. 10:14, emphasis added). When something is being made, who is in charge of the process? *The Maker*. And that's not us. Yes, we are part of the process, but we're not the one making anything happen.

In the Christian life, our focus is never to be on results. Instead it's to be on remaining. "I am the vine; you are the branches. If you remain in me and I in you, you will bear much fruit; apart from me you can do nothing" (John 15:5). Apart from Jesus we can do nothing—including being holy. So what are we called to remain in? "Remain in my love" (John 15:9). We remain in God's love when we refuse to begin striving. We remain in God's love when we stop trying to be perfect. We remain in God's love when we simply receive it.

A branch has one job: stay connected to the vine. And we have one job: stay connected to God's love. When we do so, our lives naturally produce the fruit he desires. We don't have to come up with a "do this, don't do that" list for living. When we are loved, the response of our hearts is to love in return. And when we love someone, we want to do what pleases them and brings them joy. That's why love is the fulfillment of the law.

You can't make yourself holy. You can only let yourself be loved.

God has designed certain ways for us to receive his love. Just like veins go from the vine into the branch of the tree, these spiritual practices transfer his love to our hearts.

Prayer. We receive God's love through talking to him. I've had many different conversations in the last week with friends. Some were loud and full of laughter and others quiet and serious. I would think it was strange if someone said, "You can only talk to your friends in this one particular way." And yet we often do the same with our conversations with God. There isn't one right way to pray. Just focus on connecting with God.

Scripture. God speaks to us through his Word. It's unlike any other book because it's "living and active" (Heb. 4:12 ESV). The Holy Spirit takes the Bible and makes it apply personally to our lives and situations. Because of that, there isn't one specific method of reading the Bible that is best either. Some people like in-depth study. Others like to read a verse a day and really think about it.

Fellowship. God also loves us through other believers. We tend to think of this in terms of going to church, but it's far more than that. It's sharing our lives with each other in meaningful ways. We need friends who will be "Jesus with skin on" to us. We can find that in a variety of ways.

Rest. We live in a world that tells us to "produce, produce, produce," and God is gently saying instead, "abide, abide, abide." We need rest built into our schedules so we can remember our role is simply to receive. What you *don't do* is just as important in your relationship with God as what you do.

As we engage in what's above in ways that fit with who God has made us, we remain in his love. And over time, we become more like Jesus. Not because we're striving to do so but because that's what happens when two people love each other. The closer you get to God, the more set apart from the world (i.e., "holy") you will naturally become.

God Is Merciful

The mystery is this: God is completely holy and different from us in every way, and yet Jesus became "fully human in every way, in order that he might become a merciful and faithful high priest in service to God, and that he might make atonement for the sins of the people" (Heb. 2:17).

You serve a God who knows what it's like to stub his toe, to need a nap, to eat a picnic of bread and fish under a brilliant blue sky. Your Savior has felt every emotion you do: happiness, anger, fear. I imagine he got teased by his brothers and kissed by his mama. He faced temptations and lost loved ones. He knew the feeling of the sun on his face and dirt under his fingernails. *He knows how hard it is to live in this world.*

Christ's mercy comes not just from a place of knowing but from truly *understanding.* "For we do not have a high priest who is unable to empathize with our weaknesses, but we have one who has been tempted in every way, just as we are—yet he did not sin" (Heb. 4:15). When you want to yell at your family at the end of a hard day, Jesus knows what it's like to be tempted with impatience. When your marriage feels rocky and you think about going somewhere else to get your needs met, Jesus understands the draw to skipping God's plan and going for the easier way. When insecurity follows you into the party and nips at your heels, Jesus can relate to your desire to shut everyone out so you can be safe.

In those moments, we can reach out for mercy. Yet most of the time we picture God judging us instead. We imagine him saying things like, "After all I've blessed you with! How can you even be having this thought?" So we disconnect our hearts from him in shame in the very moments we need him most. That leads to trying to be perfect on our own or giving up and choosing rebellion. But we can "approach God's throne of grace with confidence, so that we may receive mercy and find grace to help us in our time of need" (Heb. 4:16).

When you find yourself struggling, go to God and be honest with him. Tell him what's hurting you. Let him know you're weary. Share your frustrations with him. He will not tell you, "Try harder" (which is what you're likely to tell yourself if you don't go to him). He's been where you are. He's lived on this earth. He's walked in your shoes.

If you miss that opportunity and let temptation get the best of you, mercy is there too. A young woman sent me a message last night that asked, "How can God even want me after what I've done?" It's a mystery when we're so used to earning affection and approval. But God *does* want you. He not only wants a relationship with you, but he wants to use the places where you've experienced the most shame to bring him glory.

My dear friend Jacque Watkins had an affair, and for years she felt unworthy of God's love. But slowly he showed her she truly was forgiven. And then he did the unthinkable—asked her to share her story with other women. She unexpectedly did so in a cabin one evening at a retreat. Jacque says on her blog *Mercy Found Me*:

> The retreat concluded the next morning with a salvation message and communion. It had been a life-changing weekend for me—opening the door to transparency, listening to God's voice, and obeying. God is so good and gratitude filled my heart for how he met me in that meadow—how I was going home changed.
>
> As we were gathering our things and preparing to drive down the mountain, Vicky (a woman who was not yet a Christian) approached me and asked if we

could talk. *My stomach began to do flips. Had my story disappointed her? Had my failure killed her hope?* We walked a bit down the path and then she just said it, plain as day, *"I accepted Jesus this morning. . . ."*

I stopped dead in my tracks. *"Really? Vicky. That's wonderful!"* And after a long congratulatory hug, she profusely thanked me for sharing my story, because for her, it had changed everything. And what if our stories, our very lives, are made for just that . . . to change everything? For so long she'd been torn about choosing Jesus, thinking she needed to have everything "sorted out" and her life "cleaned up" and "together" first. She'd been waiting for the right time—waiting so long.[2]

I imagine Vicky had encountered many "perfect" Christian women along her journey. And only God knows, but if Jacque had held back her story and tried to appear perfect too, then the outcome of that retreat might have been totally different for Vicky. When we receive God's mercy and share that, we give others hope that they can find mercy too.

God Is Unchanging

We make a new friend on the playground, and the next week they like someone better. We commit to a company, only to hear later, "We're sorry but we don't need your services anymore." We say "I do" to a spouse, only to hear "I don't" years later. Our world of relationships is always changing—which is one reason why we strive for perfection. We believe if we can be perfect, then our hearts will finally be safe. After all, who could reject us if we're absolutely flawless?

What our hearts are really searching for is *security.* And God is the only one who can offer it to us because he's the only one who never changes. "Jesus Christ is the same yesterday and today and forever" (Heb. 13:8). Yes, he is endlessly creative in what he does and how he loves us. But his character remains. You can count on God's love to be there for you *no matter what*.

At first that throws us off. We don't even know how to act in a relationship where we don't have to think about earning approval or gaining affection. There aren't any games to play. There isn't any fear that someone will leave. As that really begins to sink in, we're transformed from the inside out, because we finally, fully feel safe.

Do you feel safe with God? That's an essential question, because if the answer is no, then fear will drive your relationship with him. "There is no fear in love. But perfect love drives out fear, because fear has to do with punishment. The one who fears is not made perfect in love" (1 John 4:18). Yes, we are to respect God and to recognize his power. In that sense we are to "fear" him. But we are not to be afraid of him. And we don't have to be because his character and love are unchanging.

Developmental psychologist Mary Ainsworth did extensive research into how children bond with their parents. She identified several different patterns. Out of those, "secure attachment" was the ideal. When children were securely attached, they were able to explore, grow, and freely learn, knowing they could always go back to their parent for comfort or help if needed. Secure attachment is formed when parents respond with love over and over again. In other words, they're unchanging. Parents who changed their responses and were unpredictable had anxious children who easily became distressed. If it's essential for human children to have parents who are unchanging in their response, how much more do we need the same from our heavenly Father?

None of us knows what the future will hold. We can't predict what the people in our lives will do. Even the best parents or friends will disappoint or fail us at times. We face uncertainty in almost every part of our lives. That can lead us to become controlling (part of perfectionism), or we can release control and find security in the only One who is unchanging.

Your heart is not made to try to control your world or the people in it so you can be safe. Doing so not only is impossible, but it will fill you with fear and anxiety. You don't have to try so hard to be sure you're okay. Instead you can rest in the One who promises no matter what may happen in this life, you will be secure forever because he will not change.

God Is Patient

I look out my office window to see a child tottering on her pink bike. Her dad holds the back of the seat and gently coaches her. He lets go and she rides a few feet before stopping in fear and saying, "I can't." He walks up to her again and leans over to grab hold of the seat again, then whispers more reassurances. This scene repeats itself until at last she pedals to the end of the street with a smile of victory on her face.

We understand that learning anything new takes patience. Our hearts smile when we see parents being tender with their children as they grow and learn. And yet when it comes to our heavenly Father, we're more likely to imagine him shaking his head in impatience and disapproval, wondering why we can't just get it right. Perfectionism demands that we perform flawlessly *now*. But God is not in a hurry. He has all of eternity. And he understands that *growth is a process, not an event.*

God knows the process of making us perfect will not be done until heaven. "Being confident of this, that he who began a good work in you will carry it on to completion until the day of Christ Jesus" (Phil. 1:6). I've heard it said that the longest journey is the one between our heads and hearts. We think because we know the right thing to do that we should automatically be able to do it—and that God expects that from us. But human beings are far more complicated than that. We're more like that little girl learning to ride her bike. We've got to try over and over again until we finally get the hang of it.

Perfection paralyzes us and makes us decide "I just won't ride a bike at all." That's especially true if we see God as a disapproving, demanding father. But not engaging in life at all is more harmful than any fall. In *If You Want to Walk on Water, You've Got to Get Out of the Boat,* author John Ortberg shares the story of Peter walking on the water with Jesus, then sinking, and says:

> Jesus is still looking for people who will get out of the boat. Why risk it? I believe there are many reasons:
>
> ○ It is the only way to real growth
> ○ It is the way true faith develops
> ○ It is the alternative to boredom and stagnation that causes people to wither up and die
> ○ It is part of discovering and obeying your calling
>
> I believe there are many good reasons to get out of the boat. But there is one that trumps them all: *The water is where Jesus is.*[3]

Yes, Peter sank. But as Ortberg asserts, he's the only one who got to experience what it was like to walk on the water with Jesus. And Peter would "sink" again many times, with the culmination of those being denying Jesus three times on the night before his death. Yet when Jesus was resurrected, he went looking for Peter and not only reassured him but reinstated him.

Peter went on to help establish the early church and according to tradition was eventually crucified upside down because he didn't consider himself worthy of the same type of death as his Savior. That kind of faith takes time to grow. It takes a lot of mistakes being made and forgiven. It takes a lot of sinking and then learning to stand tall. Most of all, it takes someone who is patient enough not to give up on us. God understands you're not perfect. You're a beautiful work in progress.

God Alone Is Perfect

An old story goes that quilters used to intentionally put flaws into their work to remind them that only God is perfect. In a craft where every stitch counts, those women were declaring, "I'm not even going to try to be perfect." While we're not going to be imperfect on purpose, it's still inevitable.

Like the errors in the quilts, when we let our mistakes and shortcomings be visible, we remind those around us that we are only human. I grew up in a denomination that often encouraged people to plaster on a smile even when they were broken. We were told not doing so could "hurt our witness." In other words, we'd make God look bad. But the opposite is actually true. When we cover up our wounds, hide our failure, and refuse to ask for help, we give the impression that we belong to someone who must not really love us. We also lead others to feel they have to hide their weaknesses as well.

When we say, "I'm broken. I'm weak. I made a mistake," then we are also saying, "I'm not God." The places we feel most vulnerable are often where God can show his love through us the most. You don't have to be afraid of being honest about who you are or what you're going through. God can handle it, and by opening up, you just might help someone else feel safe too. You will not make God look bad—you will show that he is good because he loves his children even in their most difficult moments.

There's an old story about two pots. One was perfect in every way. The other had cracks and broken places. Each day a woman filled the pots with rainwater she collected and then carried them down the path to her home. The first pot felt proud that she never leaked a single drop. The other felt ashamed, because no matter how hard she tried, she spilled a lot along the way.

One day the two pots overheard the woman talking with someone who lived nearby. The neighbor exclaimed, "The flowers along your path are so beautiful! What's your secret?"

The woman answered, "One of my pots is broken, and the water that spills out helps the flowers grow every day."

We think that we have to take what's broken and make it perfect in order to be used by God and bless others. But God thinks in a completely different way. He took what was perfect, his Son, and made him broken in order to bring us healing.

So if you're sitting there wondering if God can use you because your life is not as it should be, and your heart is aching—know that your greatest hurt will probably be your greatest ministry. Like the disciple Thomas who doubted until he touched the scars of Jesus, some people in your life need to see your broken places more than your victories.

We're all like the second pot in the story. God sees purpose in our brokenness even when we don't, and he can use it to bring forth beauty that blesses those around us.

God Is More Than We Can Even Imagine

We've touched on a few characteristics of God that directly relate to our pursuit of perfection. But he's so much more than we could ever explore in these pages. The more we know him, the more we realize that being perfect is not only impossible but it's also unneeded. *Because we're already loved.* When we truly believe that, our lives become a response to God's love and we want to do what pleases him. Yes, we struggle, fail, and fall sometimes. But ultimately we desire to remain connected to him.

King David had an intimate relationship with God. He experienced great victory in his walk with God (the battle with Goliath) and also devastating defeat (his affair with Bathsheba). He used words to describe for us what it was like to engage with God through all of those times. In Psalms we find an extensive list of descriptions about who God really is.

David uses these words to describe God in Psalms:

A refuge (9:9)	Faithful (33:4)
Just (9:16)	Good (34:8)
King (10:16)	Close to the brokenhearted
Righteous (11:7)	(34:18)
Rock (18:2)	Help (54:4)
Fortress (18:2)	Sustainer (54:4)
Deliverer (18:2)	Upright (92:15)
Shield (18:2)	Great (95:3)
Horn of my salvation (18:2)	Above all gods (95:3)
Stronghold (18:2)	Compassionate (103:8)
Perfect (18:30)	Gracious (103:8)
Flawless (18:30)	Slow to anger (103:8)
Trustworthy (19:7)	Abounding in love (103:8)
Shepherd (23:1)	Exalted (113:4)
Light (27:1)	My song (118:14)
Salvation (27:1)	Watcher (121:5)
Strength (28:7)	Shade (121:5)
Powerful (29:4)	Unfailing love (130:7)
Majestic (29:4)	Near (145:18)

What else would you add to that list based on your relationship with God?

God is . . .

_____

_____

Praise helps cure perfectionism. It reminds us of what true perfection really looks like and keeps us connected to God's love.

As I stood under the South Carolina sky that morning, I watched two shooting stars streak across the dark. I thought about how our lives are so much like that. We're here for a moment, we get a chance to shine, and we're gone. That thought didn't fill me with sadness. Instead it filled me with comfort. I sighed with relief and let the pressure roll off of my shoulders. I'm not God, and it's not my role to keep the universe running. Instead I'm a living paradox—small and yet called to big purposes, broken and yet showing God's glory, weak and yet growing stronger every day.

When we remember who God is, we regain perspective. As much as it feels like it on some days, the world is not on our shoulders; it's in God's hands. And we are too. He loves us in ways far beyond what we can even comprehend, as high as the stars, as endless as the sky. All we have to do is receive that love and respond to it. It's the simplest, hardest thing to do because everything within us wants to prove our worth and earn affection. But we can stop and fix our eyes instead on the only One who is worthy of our worship. When we look to him, we see who we truly are too. _Imperfect people who are infinitely, perfectly loved._

6

Daring to Be Who You **Already Are**

Maggie is on a quest to find true love. It's her fourth engagement, and the three before have earned her the nickname "Runaway Bride." Reporter Ike Graham (Richard Gere) is intrigued and becomes determined to learn the truth behind Maggie Carpenter's (Julia Roberts) bolts from the altar. He's convinced she's simply a fickle female.

But eventually they both realize Maggie's actions come from an entirely different place: Maggie has no idea who she really is. She doesn't even know how she likes her eggs cooked. Whatever the guy she's with at the time prefers, she tells herself that's the way she wants it too. It's no wonder she got proposed to time and time again—she transformed herself into someone else's idea of perfect every time she got a new boyfriend. But her heart couldn't withstand it, and at the last minute she'd make a run for freedom. Maggie had to figure out who she really was before she could be ready for real love.

Yes, the story above is a romantic comedy, but when it plays out in real life, it's a tragedy. We convince ourselves that someone else's idea of perfect must be who we really are. So we change the way we dress, think, and act so that they will approve of us. Most of us don't run in ways as obvious as Maggie. Instead we can spend years going through the motions to be someone we're not in the hopes that we'll be loved.

One of the most wonderful parts about knowing who God is and how much he loves us is that it frees us from trying to live up to other people's ideas of who we should be. Instead God invites us to discover who we truly are.

Who Does God Say You Are?

When it comes to God's truth about us, there are two types: universal and specific. Universal truth applies to all believers. Specific truth is about who you uniquely are. From what I've seen, it's the area of specific truth where most of us get tripped up. But before we go there, let's review what is true about all of us. (If this is an area of struggle for you, go through the list more thoroughly or read my devotional *God's Heart for You: Embracing Your True Worth as a Woman*.)

God says you are . . .

- Accepted (Rom. 15:7)
- Wonderfully made (Ps. 139:14)
- Forgiven (Ps. 130:3–4)
- Loved (1 John 4:16, 18)
- Blessed (Eph. 1:3)
- Chosen (1 Pet. 2:9)
- Free (Gal. 5:13)
- Provided for (Matt. 6:25–34)
- Enough (2 Pet. 1:3)
- Secure (John 10:28)
- Called (1 Cor. 1:26)
- Empowered (Eph. 1:18–20)
- Irreplaceable (1 Cor. 12:15–18)
- Known (1 Sam. 16:7)
- Strong (Phil. 4:13)
- Delightful (Ps. 147:11)
- Valuable (1 Pet. 1:7)
- Redeemed (Isa. 43:1)
- Victorious (Rom. 8:37)
- His forever (Phil. 1:6)

Nothing can change what's above. Those words are based not on your efforts but on what Jesus did for you on the cross. When you gave your life to him, this became your true identity. No matter what you do, none of those words can be taken from you.

Think of the words above like the foundation of a house. Every believer has the same foundation, but God builds on each one differently. He gives us specific strengths, skills, gifts, and characteristics. And it's in those personal truths where we often struggle. When we don't take time to understand who he has made us, we tend to try to make our house look like everyone else's. We do the emotional equivalent of "keeping up with the Joneses." The other day I watched a program on HGTV in which two couples competed to see which one had done a better job creating an entertainment room for their homes. My jaw dropped when I heard what each room cost: $100,000. Yet the designers and real estate agents still came in and found fault with both of them. They made comments like, "Well, this granite is a little outdated" or "It would have been better to have the light fixture over here." I found myself shaking my head and thinking, "It's just never enough."

I feel insecure about my decorating abilities, and somewhere in the back of my mind I think, "If I can just try harder, do more, or make it look like that blogger's home I admire, then my fear will go away." But that day I realized trying to be the "perfect decorator" is an endless treadmill. I could spend all of my time and money trying to meet the standards, and there would still be something that someone could find to criticize. I thought, "I'm better off having a home I love that simply expresses who I am." And it's the same with our identities too. We can spend our whole lives trying to "improve" who we are to please someone else. But we're better off embracing who God made us, enjoying it, and sharing who we are with others.

....
97

Discovering Who We Are

If you've read *You're Already Amazing* or *You're Made for a God-Sized Dream*, then you can probably guess what's coming next: we're going to talk about strengths and skills. Research has shown that it takes hearing something seven times for it to sink in, so even if you've done these exercises before, take a few minutes to do them again, because I believe they're essential to understanding who we are. If we think of who we are as a house, this is what provides the framework that holds the rest up.

Strengths are simply this: personal characteristics that can be used on behalf of God in service to others.

Find Your Strengths: 5 Minutes

Circle three strengths that apply to you.

○ Adventurous	○ Flexible	○ Positive
○ Athletic	○ Forgiving	○ Protective
○ Brave	○ Friendly	○ Reflective
○ Calm	○ Frugal	○ Reliable
○ Capable	○ Funny	○ Resilient
○ Caring	○ Gentle	○ Resourceful
○ Cheerful	○ Gracious	○ Responsible
○ Considerate	○ Hardworking	○ Sensitive
○ Courageous	○ Helpful	○ Servant-hearted
○ Creative	○ Honest	○ Spontaneous
○ Dedicated	○ Hospitable	○ Supportive
○ Determined	○ Imaginative	○ Talented
○ Devoted	○ Intelligent	○ Thoughtful
○ Easygoing	○ Kind	○ Trustworthy
○ Efficient	○ Loving	○ Warm
○ Encouraging	○ Loyal	○ Wise
○ Energetic	○ Mature	○ *Add your own . . .*
○ Fair	○ Organized	

Skills are how we express our strengths through action.

· · · · · · · · · · · · **Find Your Skills: 5 Minutes** · · · · · · · · · ·

Circle three skills that apply to you.

○ Acting	○ Decorating	○ Persevering
○ Adapting	○ Empathizing	○ Persuading
○ Administering	○ Encouraging	○ Planning
○ Advising	○ Evaluating	○ Prioritizing
○ Analyzing	○ Expressing	○ Problem-solving
○ Appreciating	○ Growing	○ Protecting
○ Assembling	○ Guiding	○ Relating
○ Believing	○ Helping	○ Responding
○ Building	○ Imagining	○ Risk taking
○ Challenging	○ Influencing	○ Serving
○ Cleaning	○ Initiating	○ Sharing
○ Collaborating	○ Leading	○ Speaking
○ Cooking	○ Listening	○ Supporting
○ Communicating	○ Maintaining	○ Teaching
○ Connecting	○ Managing	○ Training
○ Constructing	○ Motivating	○ Writing
○ Coordinating	○ Negotiating	○ *Add your own...*
○ Counseling	○ Nurturing	
○ Creating	○ Organizing	

Both our strengths and our skills provide opportunities for us to serve God and others. It's important for us to recognize them because they're given to us specifically by God to help us fulfill his purpose for us here on earth. Often our strengths and skills feel like so much a part of who we are that we don't pay much attention to them. We assume everyone must be like us or do what we can so easily do. But that's not true. And if you don't know your strengths and skills, someone else will try to tell you what they are.

In *Cure for the Common Life*, author Max Lucado says, "The devil is determined to bump you out of your strengths."[1] One of the enemy's most subtle strategies is to get you busy doing good things God never intended you to do. When we fall for that trap, we end up burned out, exhausted, and with a twisted view of God only as a master who is making our lives harder. But Jesus said, "My yoke is easy and my burden is light" (Matt. 11:30).

We breathe a sigh of relief when we read those words, and yet we often instantly think of another Scripture passage:

> Then Jesus said to his disciples, "Whoever wants to be my disciple must deny themselves and take up their cross and follow me. For whoever wants to save their life will lose it, but whoever loses their life for me will find it. What good will it be for someone to gain the whole world, yet forfeit their soul? Or what can anyone give in exchange for their soul?" (Matt. 16:24–26)

How can both passages be true? First we need to understand that when Jesus uses the phrase "deny themselves," he's not asking us to deny *who we are*. He's talking about what the New Testament describes our "sinful nature." And when he says "take up their cross," he's really saying, "take up *my* cross." Because as Galatians 2:20 describes it, "I have been crucified with Christ and I no longer live, but Christ lives in me." So the cross we are taking up is the cross of Christ. That means it's a cross of . . .

- ° grace
- ° forgiveness
- ° love
- ° hope
- ° healing
- ° joy
- ° life to the full

Here's the key: we're not only crucified with Christ, we are also resurrected with him. We're restored to who we were created to be before sin put us to death. Paul said, "Once I was alive apart from the law; but when the commandment came, sin sprang to life and I died" (Rom. 7:9). When we receive the life Jesus gives us, we are restored to *who we really are*. Being human is not bad. Otherwise Jesus could not have come as a human.

Jesus said, "What good will it be for someone to gain the world, yet forfeit their soul?" (Matt. 16:26). The word *soul* in this passage comes from the Greek word *psyche*. It's where we get our modern word *psychology*. The word *soul* is described by scholars as a word that "denotes one's inner life or actual personhood."[2] In other words, our soul is who we uniquely are as an individual—who God created us to be for this life and eternity. So when Jesus says, "Die to yourself," he's not saying, "Die to who you are." Instead he's saying, "Die to sin so you can become fully alive and who you were made to be in me."

This idea is probably twisted more than any other by spiritual authority figures who want people to do things "their way." They say, "You must do such-and-such to be a 'good Christian.'" And if someone says, "I don't want to," the easiest response is to say, "Too bad. You need to die to yourself and do it anyway." That leads people to twist their God-given identities to fit molds never intended for them. And it robs the body of Christ of what that individual was created to offer. Beware any leader who says, "You must do this," instead of, "Love God and do whatever you please."[3] Jesus said loving God is the greatest commandment. When we truly love him, we naturally want to do what pleases him.

Spiritual leaders who make "you must do it my way" statements are also suspicious of any material that helps people with personal growth. They tell others to read only the Bible because then they keep full control of its interpretation. And yes, you should use caution when you explore other sources. I even want you to think hard about everything that's in *this* book because I'm human and not perfect (which is the whole point of the book). But God reveals who we are in a variety of different ways, and we have the freedom to explore those and use them as tools. We just need to always take what we find back to Scripture and wise believers to make sure they're not leading us astray in any way.

With that being said, let's look at some other tools that can help you understand who you are beyond your strengths and skills.

The Five Love Languages

Imagine a friend in your circle goes through a crisis. As a group of you sit and talk about ways to help, several different ideas come up. Sally says, "I'll write her a note of encouragement." Ann adds, "I'll go sit with her at the hospital." Then Marie chimes in and says, "Let's put together a spa basket for her to find on her front porch when she gets home." Emily nods and says, "Let me know when you go over there to drop it off. I have a key, and I'd love to go in and clean her house for her as a surprise." Martha exclaims, "I'm so glad we can do all this, but what I want most is to just give her a big hug right now!"

Each woman above expressed a different love language in what she shared. Dr. Gary Chapman, author of *The Five Love Languages*,[4] describes the primary love languages this way (titles are his, descriptions are mine):

Words of Affirmation—"I give and receive love through written or spoken words."

Quality Time—"I give and receive love by spending meaningful time with others."

Receiving Gifts—"I give and receive love through tangible, physical objects."

Acts of Service—"I give and receive love through help and needs being met."

Physical Touch—"I give and receive love through expressing it with my body."

Jesus told us to "love one another" (John 13:34), and yet he stayed pretty vague about how we were to do that in our daily lives. We all love differently. By understanding our love language *and* those of others around us, we can serve them more effectively. And we'll understand why Marie wants to put together a spa basket while we want to write a letter—and how both are great ways to love people.

If we don't know our love language, we're more likely to fall into perfectionism by saying something like, "I wish I could be more creative like Marie. I just tend to fall back on words. I need to work harder to do other things." But if you work harder on putting together a gift basket, then who's going to cover the "loving with words" part? When we each express love using our strengths and skills, everyone benefits. Yes, there will be times when you need to step out of your preference and do what makes someone else feel loved because their language is different than yours. But being aware and making an intentional choice to do so is not the same as feeling guilty and like you should love more like the way someone else does.

It's important for us to also realize that our love language is the area where we will feel the most pressure to make what we do perfect. Sally will want to write the perfect letter and Marie will want to put together the perfect basket. But that attitude shifts the focus to us rather than the person we're serving. Focus on connection, not perfection.

If you'd like to discover your love language or learn more, you can do so at www.5lovelanguages.com.

Sacred Pathways

David connected with God when he was a shepherd out in a field with his sheep, long before he became king. His son Solomon drew closer to God through wisdom and knowledge. Years later, when the Messiah descended from David's line came, a woman named Mary would show her faith by caring for God's Son as a mother. Our relationships with God are not one size fits all.

Author Gary Thomas asserts that there are multiple ways we feel close to God and that each of us has one or two preferred "pathways." In his book *Sacred Pathways*, he says:

> Expecting all Christians to have a certain type of quiet time can wreak havoc on a church or small group. Excited about meaningful (to us) approaches to Christian life, we sometimes assume that if others do not experience the same thing, something must be wrong with their faith. Please don't be intimidated by others' expectations. God wants to know the real you, not a caricature of what somebody else wants you to be. He created you with a certain personality and temperament. God wants your worship, according to the way he made you.[5]

As he's looked into how people connect with God, Thomas has identified nine common pathways (the titles are his, the descriptions are mine):

Naturalists—"I feel closer to God when I'm outside engaging with his creation."

Sensates—"I feel closer to God when I'm worshiping with all five of my senses, such as being in a service that includes music, candles, and communion."

Traditionalists—"I feel closer to God through meaningful rituals and a disciplined life of faith that includes certain traditions."

Ascetics—"I feel closer to God through solitude and a simple life."

Activists—"I feel closer to God by pursuing justice and confronting what's wrong in our world."

Caregivers—"I feel closer to God by meeting the needs of others."

Enthusiasts—"I feel closer to God through outward expressions of emotion and celebration."

Contemplatives—"I feel closer to God by having time to focus exclusively on him and pursuing an intimate relationship with him."

Intellectuals—"I feel closer to God when I'm learning and actively pursuing growth in my life and relationship with him."

Our church small group recently explored our sacred pathways together. The results surprised us. Almost all of the men leaned strongly toward Naturalists/Caregivers pathways (yes, you can have more than one) and most of the women scored highest on the Intellectual pathway. Knowing that gave us new insight into how we relate to God as well as to each other and made our group stronger.

If none of the pathways above resonates with you, add your own. Gary Thomas's whole point is that we each have different ways of connecting with God. Yes, there are practices that are essential for every Christian, like prayer, Bible reading, and fellowship. But even those are lived out differently. For example, my Naturalist/Caregiver husband enjoyed a men's mountain biking group that did a devotional together at the end of the ride. As an Intellectual, I would rather skip the ride completely to stay curled up indoors on the couch with a new book that helped me grow. Both are valid ways to connect with God.

Yes, Jesus is "the way and the truth and the life" (John 14:6). But the ways we can connect with the one who is *the Way* are as unique as we are. Be careful of anyone who tells you that his or her way of worshiping is the only right one. And enjoy finding out more about how God created you to connect with him.

You can find out more about Sacred Pathways at www.gary thomas.com.

Personality Tests

I will never forget sitting in a campus ministry meeting and hearing the word *introvert* for the first time. Suddenly I had a way to describe my need for time by myself even though I loved being with people too. For years I had tried to force myself to be more outgoing and felt guilty when my energy tank quickly ran dry at parties. After all, I was a Christian, so wasn't I supposed to love people *all the time*? I discovered that day that God created me with specific ways of relating to others and that through them he could use me to love others just as effectively as he could use the chatty extrovert across the room.

When I talk to people about personality tests, I get a variety of reactions. Some people love them. Some people don't like them at all. But here's why I think they have a place: they give us a common language to talk about who we are and to understand each other.

The descriptions of personality types I encountered that night in college were based on four temperaments that date all the way back to descriptions offered by Hippocrates around 400 BC. They consisted of four different personalities: sanguine (pleasure-seeking and sociable, extrovert), choleric (ambitious and leader-like, extrovert), melancholic (analytical and thoughtful, introvert), and phlegmatic (laidback and peace-loving, introvert).

Over time those personality types continued to be developed, and eventually the mother-daughter team of Katharine Cook Briggs and Isabel Briggs Myers developed the best-known personality tool of today: the Myers-Briggs Type Indicator. Instead of four personality types, the Myers-Briggs asserted there were sixteen based on different combinations of four sets of letters.

You can take the Myers-Briggs test in a variety of places online, but for the sake of simplicity, I'm going to include a condensed version that will get you started thinking about your type.

Circle the letter in each pair that sounds *more* like you:

E (extrovert)—I'm the life of the party.
I (introvert)—I love people but need time alone to refuel.

S (sensing)—When I make a decision, I start by gathering information externally using my five senses.
N (intuitive)—When I make a decision, I start by listening to my internal intuition.

T (thinking)—I'm more of a thinker. I'm drawn to facts first.
F (feeling)—I'm more of a feeler. I'm drawn to emotions first.

P (perceiving)—I'm spontaneous and dislike routine.
J (judging)—I'm structured and like routine.

Now write down the combination of letters that best describes you. For example, I'm an INFJ. Even if I didn't do any more research into my type, I could know this about how God has created me:

- I'm going to need to build alone time to refuel into my schedule if I'm going to be able to effectively love people.
- If I have a decision to make, I will need time to process it internally before talking it through with others or gathering more information.
- I'm going to be drawn to work and opportunities that appeal to my heart more than my head.

○ I enjoy events and opportunities more when I've planned them in advance rather than just "seeing what happens."

What stands out to you about your personality when you read through what you chose from the options above?

_____

_____

To learn more about your personality type, go to www.myers briggs.org.

Find Your Strongest Life

Women today have *more* opportunities than ever before, and yet they are *less* satisfied with their lives. Researcher Marcus Buckingham set out to discover the reasons why. After connecting with thousands of women, he found this: most women today are not living in their sweet spots. It turns out that being who you truly are and living in it each day is more important than any demographic factor like marital status, whether or not you have children, or age when it comes to levels of life satisfaction.

With that in mind, Buckingham offers the Strong Life Test, a tool through which you can find the primary role that fits with your strengths. As you read the life roles Buckingham identifies, which one appeals most to you? (Titles are from the book, descriptions are mine.)

Advisor—"Others often look to me for my advice, and I'm able to share it in ways that make lives and situations better."

Caretaker—"I want to make sure everyone is okay. I'm in tune with those around me and will do what I can to make sure their needs are met."

Creator—"I love to discover and explore, then make something new out of what I find. I live in the world of ideas and connections."

Equalizer—"I value order and making sure people are treated fairly. I'm drawn to structure and making sure systems keep running smoothly."

Influencer—"I'm able to move people toward a particular outcome. I'm not afraid of conflict but prefer to help people get on board with where we need to go."

Motivator—"I'm aware of the energy of those around me and try to boost it whenever I can. Socializing is my favorite part of life."

Pioneer—"I want to explore new territory, take risks, and be the first to know what's coming so I can lead others in that direction too."

Teacher—"I see the potential in each person and want to pass along whatever I can to help them reach it."

Weaver—"I view the world as a web of connections, and I love helping people engage with each other and expand their social ties."

We find ourselves in many different roles in our lives: daughter, wife, mom, friend, sister, co-worker. Each of those roles comes with expectations and opportunities to try to be perfect. Buckingham suggests that by understanding the role we are called to play all throughout our lives (which will look different in each of the secondary roles above), we can become more resilient against losing who we are. And when we hold on to who we are, we live stronger, happier lives that ultimately benefit those around us more too.

I discovered the book *Find Your Strongest Life* by Marcus Buckingham at a critical time in my career. I had a job at a company I loved, but over time my responsibilities had changed in ways that had shifted me out of my primary role. When I took the test and realized I was actually a Creator, not a Weaver, I could refocus on where I could truly add the most value to the organization. And as I did so, the joy in what I did returned. The same can happen in any part of our lives—with our families, our churches, or our workplaces. It's up to us to make sure we don't get distracted by the expectations of others and end up missing why God called us to that opportunity in the first place.

You can take the Strong Life Test for free at www.stronglifetest. com.

I chose the tools above because they've been helpful to me personally and also because they focus on relationships. Through them we can better understand how we connect to each other, God, and ourselves.

When asked about the greatest commandment, Jesus answered, "'Love the Lord your God with all your heart and with all your soul and with all your mind.' This is the first and greatest commandment. And the second is like it: 'Love your neighbor as yourself'" (Matt. 22:37–39). How can we love God when we don't know how he's specifically wired us to do so? And how can we love others as ourselves when we don't even know who we are?

The wonderful part about knowing we're created by God is it means there are no wrong answers on the tools above. How he has wired you is going to be the most helpful for your unique life purpose. Resist the urge to compare your answers to others' or to wish you were different.

At the end of *Runaway Bride*, Maggie is finally ready for love. It's not because she's become the perfect woman. It's because she finally knows who she is and can freely offer herself and her affection. *Perfectionism kills love.* The two simply can't coexist. One is about performance, and the other is about relationship. One is self-focused, and the other has the courage to reach out to another. One keeps us enslaved to the standards of someone else, and the other releases us to freely offer all of who we are.

While others will tell you who you *should* be, hopefully these tools will give you words to describe who you *already* are. Ask God to show you even more about who you are—who he truly created you to be. Let him reveal the places where you've allowed the expectations of others to creep into your life and heart. Then once you know who you are, offer yourself completely to him. However you like your eggs. Whatever strengths you have. Whatever gifts he's placed within you. Yes, love God with all your heart, soul, and mind. Love your neighbor. Just remember to love yourself too.

Because you're not created to be *perfect*.

You're created to be a *person*.

7

Finding Healing in Your Relationships

I'm a little girl wading into new waters at the beach. The waves jump around me like eager puppies as my wide eyes stare up at an endless blue sky. I can taste the salty air and hear the seagulls laughing overhead, and I take a deep breath of wonder.

Then with a sudden *zap!* I feel a sting on my leg, and sharp pain begins to spread. I turn and run for the shore, startled. I'm hollering, "Dad! Mom!" long before I reach the sand. My parents take a close look at the red welts appearing and instantly know what's happened. "You got stung by a jellyfish," they say. I'm going to be okay, but it certainly has put a damper on my day. I've always seen the beach as a safe place, and now I eye the waves with suspicion.

Years after the jellyfish incident, I'm floating through cyber-space. I check in on Facebook, Twitter, and my blog. I smile as I see kind comments and encouraging words. Then *zap!* I feel a pain in my heart as I read the words of someone who has decided to sharply criticize me. I yank back my hands from the keyboard, and tears come to my eyes.

It's not the first time I've received harsh criticism in a public way. I've also watched many of my friends go through the same. And of course, any woman can recall the playground taunts from peers or the gossipy whispers in the halls of high school. One of my friends describes the experience of getting your heart stung by someone else when you didn't see it coming as being "jelly-fished." When she said that to me, I understood exactly what she meant. Don't we all?

When we begin to wade into the waters of being who we truly are, it can be a glorious experience. We feel new freedom and joy. Then suddenly we're hurt. When that happens, our first instinct is to resolve to stay on dry, lonely land for the rest of our lives. But in doing so we miss out on so much. And, ironically, that choice makes us more likely to become someone who wounds others.

So far we've talked about how the quest for perfection affects us personally. But unfortunately it doesn't stop there. It reaches its tentacles into our relationships too. I'm convinced that things like "being jellyfished," gossip, and the "mean girls" phenomenon all have ties to perfectionism.

Where It All Begins

How do we learn to act in ways that wound each other? I recently went to the park with two friends and their toddler daughters. The girls played with carefree abandon. Yes, there were a few scuffles about toys and discussions about "sharing," but no one got left out for long. When we're young, we accept each other fairly easily. Perhaps because we lack self-consciousness.

Then somewhere around early elementary school we develop a sense of "them" and "me." We understand that the world doesn't revolve around us and we have to find a way to fit into it. We start that process with our peers. Somehow kids come up with systems that determine what should be worn, said, and even brought for lunch. Suddenly there are standards that tell us what it means to be socially perfect. An image that's accepted as the ideal.

Every kid has to choose how they'll respond to the expectations of their peers. They usually do so by going in one of two directions: rebellion or conformity.

Standards for "Perfection"

It's the same kind of choice we make anytime we encounter someone who tells us what we must do to be perfect. Churches, families, and workplaces all have social systems too. While it begins in childhood, this type of dilemma continues all our lives.

When kids rebel against the standards for perfection, they may show it in obvious ways like wearing all black or listening to a certain kind of music. Those who conform do the same by wearing designer brands or making sure they sit at a certain spot during lunch. The wrestling match with "perfection" tends to be very outwardly visible in our youth. Anyone who's watching can tell which way we've decided to react to the expectations placed on us.

Parents, teachers, and other authority figures can spend a lot of time trying to change the outward signs of these responses to "perfection." They beg their kids to stop dressing a certain way or hanging out with a particular crowd. But all of those things are just symptoms. What all of us—kids or grown-ups—need is not an outer change but a brand-new system that's not designed around "perfection."

That's where Jesus comes in. Rather than starting with standards for perfection, he begins with grace and leads us into love.

When you are a child, your life is not about performance. It's about relationship. You are free to be who you are, and you know you are loved. If we're to heal the ways we relate to each other, we all must find our way back to that place of childlike faith.

The Hidden Pressure in "Popularity"

The kids who choose the way of "conformity" and are able to pull it off often get the label of "cool." They become the "popular" crowd. They're simultaneously admired and feared, sought out and gossiped about, accepted and rejected. We've put those people in a place where no human being belongs, and they can't possibly live up to what we're asking them to do: be perfect. In other words, *be an idol.*

This doesn't just happen in school. Again, every church, workplace, and organization struggles with this too. The internet and social media make the online world especially prone to placing people on pedestals. First we build them up in our minds. We strip them of their individuality and instead turn them into a symbol of what we want to be. They become a stereotype: "the perfect cheerleader" or "the perfect writer" or "the perfect mom." We try to be like them and copy their every move. We wear what they wear, shop where they shop, read the books they read.

But we realize that we can't meet those "standards," and resentment begins to build. We don't realize that person isn't meeting the standards we aspire to either—we've just created an impossibly perfect image of that individual. And when they fall short, there's only one thing to do: tear them down even more. So we gossip about the cheerleader, we criticize the pastor, we focus on the dirty floor of the neighbor down the street whom we envy.

And here's where it gets even crazier: once we've torn down that "idol," we go looking for another one. We feel compelled to keep believing "perfection" exists. Because if it doesn't, it means we don't have any hope of being perfect.

This crazy dance of coolness is where people get hurt. They get hurt when we place them on pedestals with no room for error. They get wounded when we tell them, "You'd better not let us/the church/the office down." They end up falling when we say, "You need to reach just a bit higher because I'm following in your footsteps." No one can live up to that pressure. It leads to depression and anxiety and makes leaders vulnerable to temptation as a method to cope with the pressure or to simply have a way out.

People also get hurt when we subsequently yank them off those pedestals. We say, "Well, I never thought she could do the job anyway" or "I knew their family couldn't be as together as it seemed." We feel a sick satisfaction that we're better than we thought we were. Meanwhile, the person we've idolized feels isolated and hurt and is wondering how they ever got to this place of being attacked by those who once looked up to them.

Women are the worst at this, friends. I've watched it happen over and over again. I've experienced it personally, and I imagine if you think hard enough about it you'll realize you have too. We have to stop doing this to each other.

Becoming a Safe Person for Others

When I share this message with women, I'm usually met with a resounding, "Yes! We need to act differently! I want people to stop judging me." We tend to think we've got to make everyone else change. But I've found *the only way to stop the power of perfectionism in your life is to learn to give grace to others rather than waiting for them to offer it to you.*

Jesus said, "Do not judge, or you too will be judged. For in the same way you judge others, you will be judged, and with the measure you use, it will be measured to you" (Matt. 7:1–2). Those verses have always been a mystery to me, and I'm still not sure I fully understand all they mean. But I do know this: *the system we use to judge others is the same one we use to judge ourselves.* Perfectionism is really about perspective, and if we want to be free of it, we have to change the way we see the world.

Here's how I believe we can move toward defeating perfectionism in our own hearts and healing our relationships.

Refuse to Gossip

Sherry leans over to Deb and says, "Did you hear how she raised her voice at her kids last week at the park? We couldn't believe it." Sherry and Deb shake their heads and go on to discuss the shortcomings of other moms in their circle. For a few minutes they feel better, but when they go home and make their own mistakes, guilt and shame come crashing down around them.

Gossip hurts those who speak and hear it just as much as the person you're talking about. And in essence gossip is always about a way someone has not lived up to the "standards of perfection" set by the social system they're in. The series *Downton Abbey* depicts a wealthy British household in the early twentieth century and the lives of the family members as well as the servants.

It's interesting to hear what was considered a "scandal" back in those times. If a servant dared to speak informally to a member of the household while carrying a tray of food into the dining room, it would have caused an uproar. Now we chat and laugh with waiters at restaurants like we're old friends. We think it's odd that there would ever be any difference between those at the table and those bringing the food.

But that's the point: social "standards of perfection" change based on the time period, culture, and setting. In reality they're just personal preferences of people. Most of the time gossip has little to do with sin and a whole lot to do with society. When we expect others to live up to what our culture tells us is ideal, we unknowingly trap ourselves into believing we have to do the same—or we'll face gossip too.

Even when actual sin is involved, Scripture never offers gossip as a solution. We often turn "prayer requests" into spiritual disguises for plain old gossip. If we have an issue with someone, we're to go to them one-on-one to discuss it. And if the issue isn't with us, there's no need for us to talk about it with others.

I know we don't like this as women. We're such relational creatures, and a lot of our conversations center on other people. We want to know what's going on with everyone in our lives. We just need to understand there's a difference between sharing and gossip. Something is gossip if it . . .

- ° tears someone down rather than builds them up
- ° is not something we would repeat if that person were present
- ° makes us feel "superior" in some way
- ° reinforces the "standards of perfection" of our social system
- ° discourages rather than encourages

Yes, it's hard not to gossip. But if you want to be free from perfectionism, you have to be willing to set others free too. And that means not holding them to standards God never places on them. It also means offering grace and support when they do mess up rather than seeing their failures as a way to make ourselves look better. If in doubt, don't say it. *Instead intentionally speak well of others when they're not in your presence.*

Stop Harmful Criticism

Sandra's mother-in-law runs a finger along the back of the chair and says, "I just read an article about how dust can carry germs." Sandra rolls her eyes and tries to bite her tongue, but inside she feels crushed. "Won't I ever be good enough?" she wonders. Hours later she opens the door of her daughter's bedroom and looks at the clothes scattered across the floor. Her frustration overflows and she says, "You're never going to be a good wife if you don't know how to keep your space clean!" Her daughter looks up with startled eyes and says, "I was just picking out an outfit to wear on my date Friday night. I was going to pick it all back up." Sandra apologizes and hugs her daughter, but she knows the words will leave a mark that will take time to heal. She shuts the door feeling even worse about herself than before.

While gossip is what we say about others when they're not in the room, criticism is what we say to them when they're standing right in front of us. And it has a ripple effect. We're criticized and then we criticize. After all, it's not fair if we're the only one who has to live up to the standards, right?

Criticism is a negative observation that doesn't lead to a solution. It usually comes from a place of pride, frustration, or entitlement. And it's often made about something out of our control or care. Yes, there are times we need to speak up in order to bring about changes (we'll talk about them soon), but criticism actually has the opposite effect. Instead of changing, those we criticize tend to become defensive and even more convinced that they're right.

If we get outward conformity to what we want in the moment, we're still likely to be starting an inward rebellion in that person.

Instead of criticizing, look for what someone is doing well and affirm it. Years of psychological research has shown this is a far more effective way to get people to change. *Choose to compliment instead of criticize.*

Avoid Condemning

Amy looks at her husband's dishes in the sink and then glances into the living room to find him sitting on the couch. She's had enough and marches over to tell him much more than, "Please respect me by putting your dishes in the washer like we agreed we would all do." Instead she says, "You're such a lazy slob!" Amy has just blown right by criticism straight into the dangerous territory of condemnation.

Criticism is usually about an outward action while condemnation attacks a person's character. It's a warning sign that a relationship is headed for serious trouble. When a spouse shifts from, "You leave your dishes in the sink and that needs to change" to "You're a total mess," then the marriage is much more impacted. Usually we switch to condemnation because we feel like criticism isn't working. Or we use condemnation on an entire group of people that we have stereotyped. "They" are stupid. "They" are less spiritual. "They" are mean.

Here's the trouble: "There is now no condemnation for those who are in Christ Jesus" (Rom. 8:1). *If you are condemning someone, you are siding with the enemy.* It's not your place to judge another person. "Who are you to judge someone else's servant? To their own master, servants stand or fall. And they will stand, for the Lord is able to make them stand" (Rom. 14:4). Condemnation crushes the hearts of people. It's one thing to have someone say, "Your report could be better organized next time by doing the headings this way" and quite another for someone to say, "You're a worthless employee."

Even in our sin, God doesn't ever deal with us in a condemning way. It's his *kindness* that leads us to repentance (see Rom. 2:4). And he reminds us of our true identities so that we begin to act in alignment with who we really are and who he is again. Research has verified this as well: if you want someone to change, then remind them of who they truly are. If you condemn them instead, you're only reinforcing the way they're acting. *People tend to become who you believe them to be, so always believe the best.*

Choose Encouragement

Shelly wants to share that juicy story, offer a witty criticism, or condemn that group of people who've been driving her crazy. But she decides to hold her tongue a bit more. At first she gets comments like, "You're being a bit quiet today." Shelly smiles and nods as she thinks about how this is harder than she thought it would be. But eventually she begins speaking up in a new way. As she does, the responses she gets from others are more often along the lines of, "I'm glad I got to talk to you today!"

Gossip, criticism, and condemnation have one opposite: encouragement. "Encourage one another daily, as long as it is called 'Today,' so that none of you may be hardened by sin's deceitfulness" (Heb. 3:13). Two phrases stand out to me in that passage. The first is "encourage one another daily." In other words, do it now. Don't wait until you think people have it all together, have met the standards, or have finally gotten it right. The next is "so that none of you may be hardened by sin's deceitfulness." When we refuse to encourage each other and instead tear each other down, our hearts become hard. When we encourage each other every day, we fight the lies instead and keep our hearts tender.

If you're struggling to find something encouraging to say, think through this list from Philippians 4:8 and comment on whatever is . . .

- ° true
- ° noble
- ° right
- ° pure
- ° lovely
- ° admirable
- ° excellent
- ° praiseworthy

Sometimes encouragement can be like mining for diamonds. It may take some time, but there's something worth finding wherever you are or whomever you're talking to.

What If You Do Need to Correct Something?

Alicia has come into work late four days in a row. Each time her manager, Christy, has responded. At first she just told one of Alicia's co-workers, "I can't believe she's late again. She was probably out partying." The next day she said to Alicia, "You're doing a terrible job. Watch out or we'll replace you." The next day she added, "It's clear you're lazy." On the fourth day Christy ignores Alicia being late and instead tries to compliment her on everything she does well that day. But when Alicia shows up late again on the fifth day, Christy is out of strategies. She doesn't want to discourage Alicia, but at the same time, this behavior clearly has to change.

We'll all face times when we can't simply ignore what another person is doing or offer encouragement without any feedback about what has to change. So we need to know how to do so without perpetuating the feeling for them or us that perfection is what's required. In their book *Boundaries,* Dr. Henry Cloud and Dr. John Townsend explain it this way:

> *You cannot change others.* More people suffer from trying to change others than from any other sickness. And it is impossible.
>
> What you *can* do is *influence* others. But there is a trick. Since you cannot get *them* to change, you must change *yourself* so that their destructive patterns no longer work on you. Change your way of dealing with them; they may be motivated to change if their old ways no longer work.[1]

Christy goes home from work that night to think about what she can do differently. She reaches out to another woman who has mentored her to get wisdom as well. Christy also thinks about how God treats her when she has a habit in her life that needs to change. She writes this in her journal:

- *God says I'm responsible for my words and behavior.* No matter what Alicia does, I will not gossip, criticize, or condemn.
- *God tells us clearly what he wants from us.* I will meet with Alicia and go over her hours with her to make sure she understands what's expected.
- *God also lets us know the consequences of our decisions.* I will let Alicia know that if she's late again, she'll be sent to human resources for a meeting.
- *God enforces the consequences without withdrawing his love.* If Alicia is late again, I'll let her know I care about her but I'm still setting up a meeting with human resources that she will have to attend.

There will be times when you will need to deal with something another person is doing. But even in those times, you can do so in ways that don't make you or the other person feel excessive pressure. It's okay to expect someone to fulfill their responsibilities and do their work with excellence. God does the same with us. But he does so in ways that are clear and specific and allow us to experience the natural consequences of our choices. God doesn't need to criticize or condemn us to get results. And he doesn't want to. He knows that it's love, not the law, that leads to true repentance and right actions.

How Treating Others Differently Takes Away Our Fear

If you gossip about others, you will fear being gossiped about. If you criticize others, you will fear being criticized.

If you condemn those around you, you will fear facing condemnation.

The only way to be free from the pressure to be perfect is to give people permission to stop trying so hard as well. We want to say, "Everyone just give me grace!" but then we withhold it from others. That's not how it works. Every time we expect someone else to be perfect, we send this message to our hearts: *You have to be perfect too.* We don't get to have it both ways. Either everyone in our lives gets to live by a new system, or we get to stay stuck in the same old patterns together. It all comes back to this: "In the same way you judge others, you will be judged, and with the measure you use, it will be measured to you" (Matt. 7:2). We really can make a difference in our own hearts and in the hearts of others too through the way we use our words.

What Will We Do with Our Words?

Women have told me how words have wounded them. They've walked into my counseling office and bared the scars on their hearts. They've leaned into me at blogging conferences and told of unkind comments. They've confided in me over coffee—the lines still echoing all the way back to childhood. I nod my head in understanding every time. Because I know "reckless words pierce like a sword" (Prov. 12:18 NIV 1984).

Yes, words can be weapons. A careless remark. A bit of gossip. A little insensitivity in a stress-filled moment. Do we know what we do to our sisters? I sit alone and pray about this one day when I realize I've become afraid of words—of what they can do. And it seems in the dark I sense a whisper in my heart from God: "Daughter, words can defend and protect too." It's right there in our armor: "the sword of the Spirit, which is the word of God" (Eph. 6:17). *We must choose how we wield our words.*

In my heart I once pictured the enemy coming and a wounded woman on the ground behind me. I put my sword in front of her and said, "You can't have her. She belongs to the King." I still get goose bumps as I put those words on this page—because that is why I write. Because life is hard and we all fall, and we need sisters who stand in the gap for us. Because words have the capacity to hold back evil, to bring forth life, and to sustain, encourage, and unite us.

Words are powerful. And if you think yours aren't part of a battle much bigger than you, *think again.* So what do we do with this knowing, this sword that's in our hands? Sisters, let's choose to put our words firmly on the side of the kingdom—to use them to protect and never to harm. I'm raising my sword and pledging my allegiance to you and to the One who loves us.

Will you join me?

· · · · · · · · · · *A Commitment of Words* · · · · · · · · · ·

We commit to using our words to defend and heal, not to harm.

We will not gossip.

We will not belittle.

We will guard our sisters by always speaking the best about them, encouraging them to be all God would have them to be, and offering grace instead of condemnation.

We will be loyal and loving, remembering that even if we disagree, we still fight on the same side—never against each other.

We will use our words to build up not tear down, to bring hope and not hurt.

We offer our words as a powerful weapon to fight for each other on the side of all that is good, right, and true.

. . . .

Women also tell me of how words healed them. They've walked into my counseling office and shared the encouragement planted in their hearts. They've leaned into me at blogging conferences and told of grace-giving comments. They've confided in me over coffee about the life-giving lines stretching all the way back to childhood. Do we know what we do *for* our sisters?

Your words matter. They make a difference. The choice is ours. Sisters, let's wield our words in ways that change the world . . . starting with each other.

Because when we refuse to wound each other with our words, we defeat the power of hearsay—that sneaky little deception that begins with,

"Did you hear that she . . . ?"
"Someone said that . . ."
"Well, rumor has it they . . ."

So often what follows those simple phrases are fill-in-the-blanks that have potential to wound. I've been thinking a lot about hearsay, and as I turned that word over and over in my mind, I realized it sounded a lot like another one: *heresy.*

Heresy is spreading what doesn't line up with what God says is true.

Destructive hearsay is spreading what doesn't line up with what God says is true about another person.

They're close cousins. One is about doctrine. The other is about God's daughters. I think both break his heart. Gossip, criticism, condemnation. It's so easy to get pulled into all of those. Before we even realize it, our tongues have become swords, and we slash our sisters, then wonder why we feel unsafe in relationships. *Can we please stop, friends?* Actually, we can't. Even if we make the commitment above. "No one can tame the tongue," says James 3:8 (NLT). But here's the good news: We don't have to do it on our own. Jesus, the Word made flesh, lives within us, and he can help us speak differently.

To encourage instead of criticize.

To cheer on instead of tear down.

To step forward with support instead of standing back in judgment.

My friend and fellow writer Annie Downs recently wrote a book called *Speak Love* that includes these wise words: "What we say isn't just random words flying out of our mouths but the chance to either build someone up or completely tear someone down."[2] That sentence sounds a lot like this one from Paul: "Do not let any unwholesome talk come out of your mouths, but only what is helpful for building others up according to their needs, that it may benefit those who listen" (Eph. 4:29).

Before we speak, we can ask:

○ Is this going to build someone up or tear someone down?
○ Does this help meet the needs of the person I'm talking to or about?
○ Does it benefit those who are listening?

Most of all, we can ask Jesus to guide our words so that they are a source of life, healing, and encouragement. We all struggle with this, ladies. It's part of being human. And I think women are especially vulnerable—often with good intentions. So let's help each other out too. Let's commit not to speak or listen to what can wound each other. We can do so with grace, understanding, and gentleness. But we must do it.

Hearsay.
Heresy.

Let's come up with a new word: *hersay*.

It can be a synonym for encouragement—for words spoken from the heart that make our sisters feel safe, whether we are together or apart.

God loves all of us. And he wants every single one of his daughters to be free from the trap of "perfection." You. Me. The woman you admire. The woman you criticize. *Everyone.*

The change we long for starts with us. It begins with our hearts saying to those around us, "I will not expect you to be perfect. I will accept you as you are. I will love you at your best and at your worst. I will not jellyfish you. Instead I will encourage and defend you with my words. I will show you grace and be a safe place in your life. I will help you be free. And I need you to help me."

No one has it all together.

So we're all better together.

A Practical Plan for Beating **Perfectionism**

Rachel nods her head as the speaker talks about receiving grace and not being so hard on ourselves or each other. With all her heart she whispers a prayer on the way home, "Lord, please help me learn to live differently. I don't want to pursue perfection anymore. Instead I simply just want more of you."

The minute Rachel walks in the door, her husband announces, "My parents are coming for the weekend." She looks at the dust bunnies growing into jackrabbits in the corners, and her newfound peace evaporates.

Then Rachel inspects the outfits her husband has chosen for their children that day and asks in horror, "You let them go out in public that way?"

To top it all off, a friend who seems to have it all together calls in the midst of the chaos. Rachel forces a smile into her voice and insists, "I'm fine!"

By the time Rachel lays her head down to sleep, these labels are sticking to her soul again:

"Bad wife."
"Bad mother."
"Bad friend."

Tears slip from Rachel's eyes as she confesses to the ceiling, "Lord, I want to stop trying to be perfect, but I don't know *how*." We've all had experiences like Rachel's. We truly want to be different only to find ourselves so easily slipping into old patterns. Learning new truths is a beginning, but nothing changes without action. That means it's time to get practical.

What can we actually do on a day-to-day basis to help us shift from pursuing perfection to embracing God's perfect love?

Pursue Excellence, Not Perfection

Whenever someone starts talking about how it's okay not to be perfect, I can watch the women in the room begin to squirm (myself included). Yes, we desperately want more grace and freedom in our lives. But we also have this fear that if we let ourselves off the hook, everything will just go to pieces. We won't do a good job anymore. Our parenting will be halfhearted. Our work will be shabby. Our house will get a visit from the health inspector. So let's get this clear right up front: *not being perfect doesn't mean you don't work hard and try to do well.*

We're clearly told, "Whatever you do, work at it with all your heart, as working for the Lord" (Col. 3:23). We're not to slack off, become lazy, or do less than what we can because of grace. Instead, God's love and kindness become motivation for our hard work. But we're also not told, "Whatever you do, do it perfectly."

Working "with all your heart" simply means being intentional about what we do and doing it out of love.

When we live under perfectionism, we're following a system that has this progression:

Work ———▶ Approval

But God switches the order:

Approval ———▶ Work

When we do what we do as a response to knowing we're already loved and accepted, rather than as a way to earn love and acceptance, it changes everything.

Instead of decorating her home to impress people, Alison makes her home beautiful as an expression of gratitude to God and a way to love him by sharing what he's given her with others.

Instead of double-checking the numbers to make sure she looks good, Miranda does her report with diligence because she knows that God is her ultimate authority and that integrity brings him joy.

Instead of trying to get every answer in her Bible study right so she'll seem spiritual, Cheryl looks at it as an opportunity to grow closer to God and connect with other people in new ways.

Pursuing excellence leads to joy and satisfaction. Pursuing perfection leads to burnout and frustration.

What's "excellent" can be difficult to define, though, which is another reason we tend to end up going for perfection instead. So let's take a look at that together and define excellence this way:

Excellence is doing what you can, with what you have, where you are, as you are.

It means given your circumstances, your limitations, your abilities, and other factors, you've done what you can to do well. That means an "excellent" meal when company comes and you've had time to be prepared may be homemade if you'd like. But an "excellent" meal when you and your family have the flu can be chicken soup from a can. Both are what you can realistically do at that time to meet the need. That's the most important part to remember: perfectionism is almost always self-focused; excellence lets you focus instead on what will truly benefit the other people and bring joy to God.

Practical step: Write the definition for excellence above on a piece of paper and put it somewhere you can see it at least once a day.

Accept That Not Everything in Your Life Can Be Excellent

You and a friend decide to go check out a new restaurant for lunch one day. You enter the door and the manager greets you. He says, "This restaurant is a buffet. You can have it all!" You pick and choose what you want and then take your seat at a table. Several minutes later your friend appears with numerous piled-high plates in her hands and sets them down. She says, "I'm going back for more. I'll be back soon!" You ask, "What are you doing?" She replies, "He said I can have it all, so I am!" You stare at the plates in front of you and think, "I'm not so sure this is a good idea."

In that situation, it's easy to understand why "having it all" isn't going to bring about the best outcome. But it's easier to get confused when it comes to our everyday lives. In *Happy Women Live Better*, Valorie Burton says:

> We are in a crisis. But no one seems to have noticed. As women we have more, but enjoy less. We are more educated. We have more choices. We make more money. We raise fewer children. And thanks to technology, the chores are much easier. Women today have more opportunities than any women in the history of the

world. And yet, research shows collectively we are less happy than we were 40 years ago.[1]

Even if we decide to stop trying to be perfect, we can still cling to the idea that we must be excellent in every area of our lives. But that's not possible or beneficial. Our brains are not even created to work that way. I shared in *You're Already Amazing* that our brains lose half their neuron connections by age sixteen. This seems like a bad thing, but it's actually very good. "In essence, the most vibrant connections become our strengths, and those that fade away become our weaknesses. . . . God has physically wired me with strengths that let me fulfill his purpose for my life. And he helps me do so by strategically creating certain weaknesses too."[2]

You have only so much time, energy, and emotion in your day. You must decide how to use those resources. *It's okay not to be excellent at everything.* I'm not an excellent decorator. As much as I'd like to be, it's just not going to happen. I spend too much time inside my head (which allows me to write) to be super in tune with my surroundings. I'm not outwardly observant. I finally asked, "What does my home need to be like for me to best do what I'm called to do?" For me, that means having a simple, clean home free of clutter with a few pretty things that are meaningful to me. So I organized my closets, got some help cleaning, and had friends help me pick a few photo frames. My house is not going to win any decorating awards. But it works for me and allows me to focus on the areas where I know I need to be excellent.

When you think of an area of your life, ask yourself:

What is the ideal? (Example: A home that looks like it's out of a magazine.)

What is the minimum? (Example: A home that's sanitary and safe.)

What is the "good enough" in the middle? (Example: A home that's functional and comfortable.)

Then go for "good enough" as often as you can in as many areas as you can. *You will only be able to be truly excellent in about one to three areas of your life.* Excellence takes time, energy, passion, and long-term commitment. So it's simply not possible to have excellence in more than that many.

To determine which areas you will pursue excellence in, ask yourself:

What do I believe God has put me on earth to do that no one else can? (For example, no one else can be a mama to your children or create the art you do.)

Really reflect on your answer to that question. We spend a lot of time pursuing excellence in areas that someone else can do. For example, someone else can clean your house. That may not be a financial possibility for you right now, and that's okay. If so, I'd still say that's an area where you can choose "good enough" rather than "excellent." Then invest the time and energy you save in what you're truly called to do.

When you intentionally choose not to be excellent in an area, it's not a failure; it's wisdom. It's using your one life well. God is not concerned with you getting every last dust bunny. But he does care deeply about how you invest the strengths, skills, and gifts he's placed within you. When Paul introduces 1 Corinthians 13, the well-known "love chapter," he precedes it with the words, "I will show you the most excellent way" (1 Cor. 12:31). *Love is the most excellent way to spend your life.* And doing so as only you can brings joy to God's heart and the hearts of those around you.

Practical step: *Pick one area of your life that you will let simply be "good enough" for this week.*

Learn to Know What You Need and Ask for It

Jamie looks at the stacks of papers on her desk and wonders, "How am I ever going to get this done?" A co-worker stops by and says, "Hey, you look stressed. What do you need?" Jamie knows this person could help and briefly considers sharing. But then she tells herself she needs to pull her weight—even though this is a load too heavy for one person to carry. So she forces herself to smile and responds instead, "Nothing. I'm fine, thanks."

Abby just had a new baby and feels like the walls of her house are closing in on her. All she really wants is a nap and a shower. She thinks about her excitement during pregnancy and feels guilty that since her little one has arrived, her enthusiasm isn't as intense. A friend texts her and says, "How are you doing? Can I bring you anything or sit with the baby for a while?" Abby wants to reply, "I'm exhausted and lonely. I'd love some lunch and a chance to get some rest." But she glances in the mirror at her weary reflection and post-pregnancy weight, then texts, "I'm good! Thanks for asking!"

Haley's husband decided that a younger woman would make his life more exciting. He emptied Haley's heart as well as her bank account before he left. A friend at church who works in finance senses she may be struggling. She stops Haley on Sunday morning and says, "You've had a big life change and I care about you. I can help you figure out what this means for your financial future." Haley desperately wants to say yes, but she thinks of her credit card bill and her cheeks flush with shame. She has to get that taken care of before she can let this woman see anything. "Thank you," she says. "I just need more time to figure a few things out, then maybe I'll be in touch."

If perfectionism could be identified by one phrase, it would be this: "I'm fine." We falsely believe being perfect means not needing anything. But we're not God and we're *always* in need. *Every single one of us.* Even that woman you think has it all together. None of us are self-sufficient. We're not supposed to be. God created us to need him and each other.

One of the hardest parts of overcoming perfectionism is raising our hands, opening up our hearts, and simply saying, "I need help." A friend of mine recently went through a difficult time, and as several of us gathered around her to offer support, she kept saying, "I'm not allowed to be broken." How many of us have felt that way? I certainly have. This friend is incredibly kind and generous. If you need anything, she's there. So we gently asked, "How does it make you feel when you help us?" She looked up with tears in her eyes and said, "It's good. It makes me feel valued and loved." We responded, "Then give us the gift of helping you now."

This is the incorrect belief we have to change: *if we need help, we're a burden.* Because the opposite is true. In the kingdom of God, it's more of a blessing to give than receive. So when we're in need and we let someone help us, we're blessing them.

The problem is, this gets twisted in our minds because we've all known people who take advantage of the kindness of others, and we would never want to be one of them. When I worked as a counselor, I certainly experienced this. Some clients walked in motivated to change and worked hard. Others wanted to sit back and let everyone else change. To set your mind at ease, let's talk about how you can do a quick motive check and be confident asking for help.

Before you reach out for help, ask yourself:

What do I really need? It helps to identify and be able to share a specific solution. It can be overwhelming if we simply declare, "I'm exhausted and can't take this anymore." Instead we can say, "I need a friend to come over for an hour to watch my baby so I can take a shower and grab a few minutes of sleep." If you're not sure exactly what you need, just make a guess. Something is better than nothing.

What can I take responsibility for myself, and where do I need some help to share the load? We do need to care for what God has entrusted to us, but none of us can do that alone. It's okay to be human, have limits, and ask for support. For example, "I'm doing what a new mama should—which is feeding my baby and changing her diapers. I need some extra rest and help with other things so I can continue doing so without becoming completely exhausted."

What is my motivation? Am I asking for this as a gift, or do I feel entitled to it? No one has to meet our needs. We are always free to ask for help and they're always free to say no. For example, "I watched Bridget's baby for her, so she has to do the same for me or I'm going to be mad" isn't helpful, while, "I know Bridget is tired and busy too, but I'm going to see if coming over for an hour this afternoon works for her. I'd be so grateful!"

What does God say about this? Am I going to a source God has provided, or am I seeking to meet this need outside of his boundaries? We can choose to meet legitimate needs in illegitimate ways. For example, "I will ask my husband if we can talk for a few minutes tonight so I can process some of this stress with him" instead of "My husband hasn't been as attentive as I'd like since the baby came, so I'm going to write a long email to my ex-boyfriend from high school who seems more understanding."

We're called to be in "one another" relationships. That means God intends for us to give sometimes and receive other times. We can get into unhealthy patterns of always giving or always receiving. Instead our connections with each other are to be about both. When we try to be perfect, it shuts down our capacity to receive. And when we do so, we unknowingly shut others out too.

Think about a time when you were able to be genuinely helpful to someone. You probably felt affirmed and valued and got a little boost of happiness. The same happens to those you love when you let them give to you. Research has shown that altruism is one of the best ways to build well-being in our lives. So don't deprive those around you of those benefits just because you're afraid of what they may think of you. Give others the gift of helping you. You need it—and they need to see you're not perfect because it sets them free to ask for help and grace too.

Practical step: Ask for help in one small way this week.

Live with Gratitude

My friend and fellow writer Ann Voskamp took a dare to write down one thousand gifts in her life. That list pulled her out of a season of depression and awakened her in new ways to God's presence. She says, "All gratitude is ultimately gratitude for Christ, all remembering is a remembrance of him. For in him all things were created, are sustained, have their being."[3] Gratitude is like kryptonite to perfectionism.

Perfectionism says, "It's not enough."
Gratitude says, "It's more than enough."

Perfectionism says, "I'm lacking."
Gratitude says, "I'm living in abundance."

Perfectionism says, "God is holding out on me."
Gratitude says, "God is good and gracious."

Perfectionism says, "I must try harder and go farther."
Gratitude says, "I will be fully present in this moment."

When the apostle Paul said he had "learned" to be content, surely gratitude was part of that process for him. It turns out giving thanks not only connects us to God but increases our day-to-day happiness as well. Researchers did an experiment with three groups. The first wrote down five things they were grateful for each week. The second group wrote down five challenges they faced. And the third simply wrote down five random events. Those who recorded five blessings increased their happiness by 25 percent over their baseline level.[4] That's a significant amount!

Counting our blessings seems like such a simple task, and yet it can be hard to find a way to actually make it happen. So let's talk about some tools that can help you do so:

- **Old-fashioned pen and paper by your bedside**—Record one blessing every night before you turn out the light, and you'll have more than five by the end of the week.
- **Ann Voskamp's One Thousand Gifts App**—You can download this for free on your smartphone. It lets you record your gifts and include photos as well.
- **Dinnertime prayers**—Instead of asking the blessing, say thanks for a blessing each time you pray together as a family before a meal.
- **Make gratitude part of your decor**—Make or find a simple "Give thanks" sign and put it in a spot where you'll see it each day (bathroom mirror, refrigerator door, on your garage wall where you pull in your car).
- **Gratitude journal**—Keep a small notebook in your purse and jot down a couple of words when you find a blessing in your day.
- **Get a gratitude buddy**—One thing that can make it hard to be grateful is feeling like sharing our blessings might make someone else feel bad. Ask a friend to be your designated gratitude buddy who you always know you can share happy news with—and vice versa.

These are just ideas as starting points. The best plan is the one you will enjoy and actually do. There's no right or wrong way to incorporate gratitude into your life.

You can also use gratitude as a perfectionism-fighting tool right in the middle of stressful moments. When you begin to feel anxious, your brain has flipped on the "fight-or-flight response." To get your mind to calm down, you need to replace those fear-based thoughts with new ones. Saying thanks is a simple way to start doing so.

For example, if you're walking into a party and hoping to make a perfect impression, you may instantly start worrying that your outfit doesn't look cute enough. Instead you can look at each person and say thanks for them by name: "Thank you, God, for Amanda. Thank you, God, for Emma. Thank you, God, for Veronica." If you run out of names, just keep on going. "Thank you, God, for cheese dip" is an acceptable prayer!

Because gratitude goes against the way our brains are used to thinking, it feels awkward and fake. So know it's okay if you don't feel it when you're saying thanks. There's nothing wrong with you and it still counts. It just takes time for us to create new neural pathways in our minds. You don't have to be perfect when it comes to practicing gratitude either.

Practical step: Pick one of the gratitude ideas in this section and try it for one day.

Treat Life Like an Experiment, Not a Test

"I want to begin a new project," she says. "Actually, I've wanted to for years. But I'm not sure how to do it exactly right. There are so many options. How do I know which one is best?"

I reply, "You won't know until you try. You've done a reasonable amount of research, and now it's time to just give it a shot. If what you do works, do more of it. If it doesn't, try something else."

The lines above are what I say to life coaching clients more than anything else. *Life is not a test. It's an experiment.* To grow and learn, you have to just *do something* sometimes and see what happens. When we're trying to be perfect, we don't give ourselves this freedom. We think we need to have everything figured out and be sure we can execute our plan flawlessly before we ever take a step. I wonder how many books have gone unwritten, how many races uncompleted, how many relationships never started because of false beliefs. There is no way to do anything perfectly in this world. You're going to mess up. I guarantee it. There is always risk. And the only way to deal with that is to increase your tolerance to things not going the way you planned.

If you're not ever making mistakes, you're not getting out of your comfort zone enough. Push until you fail. Then pull back a bit, learn some more, and try again. That's how growth happens. In the parable of the talents in the Gospels (see Matt. 25 and Luke 19), a master leaves his servants with resources to invest. The only servant who is rebuked is the one who hides what he's been given out of fear. The master doesn't say, "Well, at least you didn't lose what I gave you." *God doesn't expect us to be perfect, but he does expect us to try.*

What risks do you really want to take but are holding back from out of fear? I'm not suggesting jumping out of planes or acting foolishly. We do need to be diligent in our preparing and planning. But at some point, it's time to act. You will probably not get it right the first time. Maybe not even the tenth. But every time you will be getting better, stronger, and braver. Learn to make taking risks a part of your life.

Before you think I'm fearless, here's a confession: I'm not a crafty kind of girl. Nothing strikes terror in my little heart like a hot glue gun. So what am I doing next week? I'm planning to make a wreath with some friends. Not because I think my wreath will be awesome. Based on past experience, my biggest contribution will be making everyone else feel better about their skills. Nope, I'm doing it because I need to show myself once again that

I will not die just because I can't make something pretty. And I will be scared out of my wits the entire time. But I need to build my risk tolerance.

Silly example? Yep. But that's the point. Taking risks doesn't have to be some big, life-altering event. It can be choosing courage in the small things. Even craft projects. Then when there is something really big God wants you to do, you've got those perfectionism-fighting and fear-resisting muscles already built up.

Practical step: *Do something that scares you a little this week—even if everyone else thinks it's fun and easy.*

Find People Who Care More about Being Real Than Being Perfect

We don't want to see the vacuum lines in your carpet. Instead we want to hear about what's causing those worry lines to crease your forehead. We don't want to be impressed by your cute shoes. We want a glimpse of your soul. We don't want to read your "I've got it all together" blog post when we know that inside you're falling apart.

In a classic children's story called *The Velveteen Rabbit*, a toy bunny longs to become "real" too and asks another toy in the nursery about it.

> "Does it happen all at once, like being wound up," he asked, "or bit by bit?"
>
> "It doesn't happen all at once," said the Skin Horse. "You become. It takes a long time. That's why it doesn't happen often to people who break easily, or have sharp edges, or who have to be carefully kept. Generally, by the time you are Real, most of your hair has been loved off, and your eyes drop out and you get loose in the

joints and very shabby. But these things don't matter at all, because once you are Real you can't be ugly, except to people who don't understand."[5]

Becoming real is a lifelong process. But we can look for those who are actively pursuing it and invite them into our lives. That's especially true when it comes to women who are further along in the journey than we are. My friend and fellow writer Jennifer Watson said, "I would much rather hear from a 50-something, or older, who is killing it and more beautiful than she's ever been because she knows what really matters in life, not some woman afraid of aging squeezing into skinny jeans who is terrified that she's no longer relevant and useful. Every day is a battle and we are nothing without each other. Maybe it's time to stop comparing and join forces."[6]

Who are you letting speak into your life? We need peers, mentors, and encouragers. And in all of those roles, we need people who are willing to say, "I don't have it all together. But I believe we're better together."

Look for these characteristics in "real" people:

- Willing to share their struggles
- Can laugh at themselves
- Committed to facing fear and taking risks
- Get back up when they fall
- Pursue lifelong growth
- Quick to encourage others
- Celebrate the successes of those around them
- Ask for help when they need it
- Avoid gossip, criticism, and condemnation
- Embrace their weaknesses as part of who they are
- Don't apologize for their strengths but instead use them
- Love freely because they know how to freely be loved

Of course, we're all works in progress. No one is going to fit this list completely. But if you find someone going in this direction, ask if you can walk beside them. Be open to what you can learn. Honor and respect those with more life experience rather than pretending you know it all. We need each other.

Also remember you can *be* one of those people for others. If people around you seem to constantly try to be perfect, it may be because in some way you're giving off the impression they need to be. Or you may be modeling that behavior by expecting perfection from yourself. Sometimes we have to be the first one to say, "I'm struggling with this." That takes courage, but when I've done so, the response usually has been a huge sigh of relief followed by, "Me too."

There are no perfect people. We're all mixed-up, in-need-of-grace, learning-every-day people. You. Me. All of us. The good news is we're also made new, deeply loved, extraordinary women who have so much to offer the world.

Practical step: Think of one person in your life who cares more about being "real" than being "perfect." Make plans to connect with that person in the next month.

When we decide to make a change in our lives, perfectionism says we have to do it all right now. But that's not how growth happens. Growth is little by little. If you have been trying to be perfect for a lifetime, it's going to take some time to realign your thinking. That's okay. *Try to resist the urge to be perfect at not being perfect.* Just get up each day and do what you can, with what you have, where you are. And always begin by asking for God's help. Like we talked about before, what matters most is simply staying connected to him.

As you move forward, pay attention to what else triggers your perfectionism as well as what helps you overcome it. Then come up with your own ideas for adjusting those areas of your life. Think of one simple thing you can do differently and then give it a try. Overcoming perfectionism is a process. All you're really looking for is that you're moving forward in it. Inch by inch. Day by day. Year by year.

Then one day you'll find that your quest for perfection will be over because you'll be home in heaven forever. And everything will be perfect—including you. There's a reason why the desire for perfection is in your heart and why it won't go away. It reminds us that this life is not all there is. Instead of letting that longing for what's perfect lead you astray, let it do what it's intended to— which is to point you toward home and the only true "happily ever after" waiting for you there.

9

A New Perspective That Will **Change Your Life**

When we begin taking new steps toward grace, we often find ourselves getting tripped up by sneaky old perspectives.

A whisper comes into your heart that says, "Surely by now you should be able to get this right." You silently agree and promise yourself that you will try harder. After all, isn't that what God expects?

The booming voice comes from the pulpit and echoes through the sanctuary of the church. "Be perfect, therefore, as your heavenly Father is perfect" (Matt. 5:48). The people in the pews cringe but then nod.

A group of women stand around and talk about their week. Gradually and subtly it becomes a competition over who can be the most spiritual. Everyone walks away feeling more discouraged.

Maybe you can relate to the examples above, or they may have brought others to mind. All of them have this in common: legalism. That's a fancy way of describing our tendency to live by rules rather than grace—to put ourselves back under the old system that existed before Jesus came to set us free from the law. *Legalism is always part of perfectionism.*

We're all vulnerable to legalism as humans. We like rules and having a system for knowing we're doing "better" than others. And on the surface, it can seem so good or even "biblical." But we need to take a closer look at assumptions we've made, false beliefs we've adopted, and myths we've been told that may not accurately reflect God's heart. Then we can replace them with what's really true so we can walk in freedom and love the way God intends.

A New Perspective on Perfection

Let's start with the verse that seems to apply the most pressure to be perfect: "Be perfect, therefore, as your heavenly Father is perfect" (Matt. 5:48). These words appear pretty clear on the surface. It sure sounds like we have to be perfect at all times, act in exactly perfect ways, and do only perfect things. There's a perfect standard and we're called to meet it on our own, right? That seems to be the logical conclusion. Unless we're missing something here. Something really important called *context*.

We enter a danger zone when we start quoting verses of Scripture in ways that disconnect them from their context and distort their true meaning. When the enemy tempted Jesus, he quoted Scripture too. In other words, what he said was "biblical," but it was an inaccurate expression of God's heart.

Sadly, we can knowingly or unknowingly do the same by quoting verses of Scripture like the one above to "guilt" others (and ourselves) into changing outward behavior. But when we look closer at Matthew 5:48, we find Jesus's purpose in those words was exactly the opposite. To be free from the pressure to be perfect, we need to understand the true meaning.

Let's picture the scene together. "When Jesus saw the crowds, he went up on a mountainside and sat down. His disciples came to him, and he began to teach them" (Matt. 5:1–2). The words Jesus shared next became some of the best known in all the Gospels: the Sermon on the Mount. While these passages are familiar to most of us now, they were quite outrageous at the time. Jesus takes the law the Jews have tried to follow so faithfully and says in essence, "Outward behavior isn't enough. It's about your heart."

He says murder is not just about an act but an attitude.
He says adultery is not just about sex but how we see.
He says justice is not just about punishment but the way we love people.

Jesus sums up all of this with the "be perfect as God is perfect" verse. In other words, "Be perfect not just on the outside but on the inside—in your heart." There's only one logical response to that statement: "That's impossible." Those listening already know they can't even keep the external requirements of the law. They have to go to the temple to make sacrifices for their sins. But be perfect on the inside too? Be like God? There's simply no way that can happen. And that's exactly what Jesus wants them to realize, because he's there to tell them they need a Savior.

Let's also look at what comes right after the statement Jesus made about "being perfect." He follows those words up with, "Be careful not to practice your righteousness in front of others to be seen by them" (Matt. 6:1). Jesus knows that although on one hand the people know perfection is impossible, their minds are still buzzing with new ways to meet these requirements. "I'll try hard," they're probably telling themselves. "I'll make sure I do it right." And Jesus blows that away too, because he is here not to give them new laws but to offer a new way of living.

Jesus even says earlier, in Matthew 5:17, "Do not think that I have come to abolish the Law or the Prophets; I have not come to abolish them but to fulfill them." It's just that the fulfillment Jesus has in mind is completely different than what the Jewish people, especially the Pharisees, have been striving for all their lives. Jesus will fulfill the law by dying on a cross and taking all of our sin on him, every single broken law, and then in return giving us his righteousness and identity. That is the only way we can "be perfect as God is perfect."

> We don't need a new system; we need a Savior.
> We don't need to try harder; we need to trade our identities for his.
> We don't need to follow rules; we need a relationship with God.

Jesus alone can make us perfect in God's eyes. He does so in two very different ways that are both captured in Hebrews. Let's first look at Hebrews 10:14: "For by one sacrifice he has *made perfect forever* those who are being made holy."

What Jesus did through his death and resurrection means that when it comes to our identity, we are a new creation and we are already "perfect." That's because when we give our lives to Jesus, he gives us his righteousness. That is the only way we can ever have a relationship with a holy God. We can never, ever be perfect enough on our own. To get into heaven, we must be made perfect by Christ.

Yet we all know that between here and heaven, we continue to mess up. That's where another verse in Hebrews comes in: "Let us run with perseverance the race marked out for us, fixing our eyes on Jesus, the pioneer and *perfecter of faith*. For the joy set before him he endured the cross, scorning its shame, and sat down at the right hand of the throne of God" (12:1–2, emphasis added).

Who we are in our identity has been made perfect by Jesus once and for all. But our behavior is in the process of being perfected in him day by day. The first verse we looked at in Hebrews describes it as "being made holy." This is the part where we can begin to think we need to try really, really hard. But the burden of perfecting ourselves doesn't rest on our shoulders either. Jesus is our perfecter, and "he who began a good work in you will carry it on to completion until the day of Christ Jesus" (Phil. 1:6).

So here's a quick summary: *we're given a perfect identity through Jesus when he becomes our Savior, and then we grow in perfection as we surrender more and more of our lives to him.*

If that made you scratch your head a bit, you're not alone. Our culture tends to think about being perfect so differently than God does that we can easily get confused. We see perfection in our behavior as a right now, all-or-nothing type of requirement. But God's idea of perfect is entirely different than ours. "In the New Testament, the Greek word for 'perfect' is *teleios*, and it's actually more accurately described as maturing growth or completion. For example, an oak tree is the *teleios* of an acorn. [Perfection in our behavior] is also a process that will only be complete in heaven."[1] When Scripture tells us Jesus is the "perfecter" of our faith, it is also saying he's the "completer."

That means right now, all-or-nothing "perfection" as we tend to define it in human terms is actually in opposition to much of what God desires for us. The enemy of our souls knows that. He understands that if he can convince us that life is all about being perfect right now, then we'll think we're being "good Christians" while we're actually missing out on what it means to be in love with Jesus and live to the full like he promised.

Whew, that is some heavy theological stuff. Let's take a quick break and look at a down-to-earth story that will help shed some more light on how this all works. In the movie *The Princess Diaries*, Mia Thermopolis (Anne Hathaway) is an awkward teenager enduring the usual difficulties of high school. That all changes the day her paternal grandmother Clarisse Renaldi (Julie Andrews) arrives with shocking news. It turns out that Mia is far from ordinary. She is, in fact, a princess and the only heir to the throne of Genovia. Mia proceeds to get herself into a series of mishaps and embarrassing situations as she seeks to become the person she rightfully already is.

We are a lot like Mia. Her identity as a princess was secure even if she had some learning and growing to do. And our identity as perfect daughters of the King is secure even though we have a lot of the same to do too. *We are eternally perfect women who are in the process of being perfected on this earth.* We'll talk more about that as we move forward. What matters most is understanding this: we can't make ourselves perfect—either in our identities or our behavior. Today, tomorrow, and for eternity, Jesus alone is in charge of our perfection. Mia's grandmother loved her as she was yet also saw all she could become and encouraged her to embrace it. That's true of us too. Jesus loves you as you are right now in this very moment. And he's also committed to walking every step with you between here and heaven as you learn to live out who he has already declared you to be.

How We Got So Mixed-Up about Perfection in the First Place

As we return to what Jesus said that day in the Sermon on the Mount, there's more we need to explore to have full context. To understand any word, we also need to look at the culture using it. When Jesus said, "Be perfect," he did so to a group of people living in an agricultural society.

A woman hearing the word *perfect* might have thought of the bread she kneaded and then baked to feed her family. The bread wouldn't have resembled the white, neatly packaged, every-slice-the-same kind we see in stores today. Instead it would have bumps and ridges, uneven places, perhaps even a hole or two where air had pushed through the surface. Yet as she saw her family enjoying it, she would likely have said, "Perfect." Because that bread was whole and complete—it had fulfilled its purpose.

Someone else in the crowd might think of the lump of clay waiting back at his shop to be molded into a vessel for a customer. As he eyed varying options for which piece of clay to choose, all of them would have been different colors, shapes, and sizes. Yet one would call out to him as if to say, "Pick me!" and he would consider his project before reaching for that clay and thinking to himself, "Perfect." That clay could be used, and he wasn't concerned about its current state. He would shape it into what it needed to be.

Jesus himself was trained as a carpenter. In his time, he would have done all of his work by hand. The wood he handled wasn't cut by machines into uniform pieces. It was selected, sized, and turned into items by an individual. No two creations of Jesus would have been the same. The wood would have splinters and knotholes and would vary in shade and texture. Yet I can imagine him stepping back from a completed piece of work and saying, "Perfect." Not because it was flawless but because it was beautiful and useful.

Contrast those examples with how we tend to think of perfection in our world today—especially in Western culture. In the last couple of hundred years, society has shifted from farms to factories. We've switched from small, local shops to huge corporations. We've replaced much of human service with systems. The goal is efficiency, consistency, and maximum volume. Something is considered perfect when it can be duplicated over and over again. A car. A watch. A meal at a chain restaurant. Plastic surgery is another example because it's an attempt to change our individuality so that it conforms to a cultural standard instead. We try to become a "copy" of whoever is on the cover of the latest fashion magazine.

Our modern technology has significant implications for how we see perfection because much of it directly contrasts how human beings are created to live. We are not duplicates—we are one of a kind. We don't operate on flawless systems—we grow in ways that are messy and require risks and mistakes. We can't stay static—instead we continue to change until the day we die. If God wanted a world filled with people who all looked like they came from the same factory, he would have made it that way. He could have programmed us like computers. He could have chosen for us to look identical to each other. He could have had us hatch from eggs as instant grown-ups and skipped the whole messy process of birth through maturity. But he didn't.

When we read the words of Jesus in our current context without considering where they came from, we can easily apply a human definition that God never intended. And that definition varies with each one of us. What we consider to be perfect is made up of experiences, standards set by authority figures, and assumptions we may have carried with us for years. So let's pause for a moment together and explore how you personally think about perfection.

What's your definition of perfection? Take a moment to put it into words. Being perfect means . . .

Now pause and ask God if what you wrote lines up with his heart or is more of a reflection of our culture.

What is your understanding of God's definition of perfection?

After looking at the verses about perfection in Scripture, the best definition I can come up with for how God sees it when it's applied to behavior in our daily lives is simply this: *perfection is the process through which we become more mature, whole, and complete.*

In order for that to happen in our lives, five core elements are needed:

Growth—Every living thing is intended to grow. Only machines and dead things don't grow. Yet growth never aligns with our Western definition of perfect that says everything must stay the same. It's a messy, wild, lifelong process that comes with its share of mistakes and suffering. When we reject growth so that we can be perfect, we never reach our full potential. Here's the difference between growth and perfectionism:

Perfectionism is all or nothing.
Growth is little by little.

Perfectionism is all about the goal.
Growth is more about the journey.

Perfectionism is about outward appearances.
Growth is about what happens on the inside.

Perfectionism is about what we do.
Growth is about who we're becoming.[2]

Usefulness—When we think of what would have been considered perfect in the time of Jesus, all of those things have this in common: *they are fulfilling the purpose for which they were created.* The bread feeds a family. The clay becomes a pot. The wooden table provides a space for daily life to happen. When you do what God asks you to do today, you are useful to him. He knows you may be able to do more tomorrow as he continues to develop you into all you're created to be. But when you simply do what you can now, it is enough.

Service—One of the greatest ways we twist "perfection" is to make it about us. We think if we have the perfect body, house, or family, then others will accept us. But the process of perfection in Scripture is never about us. Instead it's a way that we love God, others, and ourselves. We want to continue in the process of perfection because it means we're aligning more and more with the ways God wants us to live. When we do so, we bring him joy, bless others, and find personal fulfillment too.

Surrender—When anything is made perfect, it must give itself over completely to the hands of another. That's true of wheat, clay, wine, wool, and all the other materials that would have been commonly known to the people listening to Jesus speak. The process of perfection requires that we stop trying to complete it ourselves. Instead we learn to be led by the Spirit and let God direct that process in our lives. "The LORD will perfect that which concerns me" (Ps. 138:8 NKJV).

Time—Anything in which we see any element of perfection has taken time, be it a beautiful work of art, a delightful meal, or an achievement that's admired. Living in an industrial society makes us think perfection in an instant is possible. Pop it in the microwave. Churn it out on the assembly line. Replicate it in record time. That kind of thinking sees perfection only as an outcome. But it's a lifelong journey. Look at what God is perfecting and you will see years of love and tender care.

Perfectionism is dangerous because it makes the goal of our lives being perfect rather than focusing on what Jesus said matters most—loving God, others, and ourselves. We don't have to live under the pressure to make ourselves perfect anymore. Instead we can live in the presence of One who loves us more than we can ever comprehend and has truly set us free.

The Western definition of perfection has consequences. One of the most depressed nations in the world is America.[3] In fact, depression is sometimes referred to as the "disease of industrialized nations." Researchers continue to search for the reason that's true, but one strong theory is that our cultural ideals set us up for failure. We have unrealistic expectations for ourselves, and whatever we achieve never seems like enough. We can always be thinner. We can always make more money. We can always be just a bit more spiritual. In other words, maybe someday, somehow, we can be perfect.

Developing countries don't seem to struggle with this as much. They focus more on relationships and enjoying everyday life. Yes, they have their own challenges, but when it comes to striving for perfection, those of us in richer nations are much more vulnerable. Those other nations are closer to what life was like when Jesus spoke the words we've been looking at in this chapter. Can we redefine what perfection means? Can we see it not as a demand but as a process that's full of love?

The New King James Version of Matthew 5:48 reads a bit differently. Instead of "Be perfect," it says, "You shall be perfect, just as your Father in heaven is perfect." You *will* be perfect. But not here. Not now. Not tomorrow either. Only in heaven. And even then, it won't be because of what you've done but because of what Jesus has done for you. That means you're free to enjoy the adventure of "being perfected" until that time. That journey isn't about rules, condemnation, or guilt. It's a process full of grace and joy, growth and freedom, learning and love. It will make you more of who you are, not less, and will lead you into all God has for you.

10

The Perfect Place
You're Heading One Day

"No matter how much I move toward grace and acceptance, there's still this part of my heart that longs for perfection. I look around at this world and my life sometimes and think, 'This is not how it should be.'"

I smile at my friend and then reply, "Good."

She laughs. "Good? I thought all this time we were trying to get rid of my desire for perfection!"

I answer, "We're trying to move past our attempts at attaining perfection in this life. But we will always have a desire for perfection in our hearts. It belongs there."

Our stories begin in Eden—a perfect place. Can you imagine waking up there? Everything around you is beautiful and completely alive. So are you. You have a passionate, intimate relationship with your husband. You do meaningful work. And you literally walk with God each day. Then suddenly that perfection is lost. Yet God leaves the desire for it still in your heart to remind you of what you were truly made for in the beginning.

God seems to relentlessly be leading us back toward a place like Eden. He brought the Israelites out of Egypt into a Promised Land. "So I have come down to rescue them from the hand of the Egyptians and to bring them up out of that land into a good and spacious land, a land flowing with milk and honey" (Exod. 3:8). In a culture where milk and honey are available at every grocery store, the true meaning of this description often escapes us. When we look closer, it becomes clear that "cream" would be a more accurate understanding of "milk." And while syrup would often be watered down in ancient times, honey represented true sweetness. God is saying, "I'm bringing you to a place that's not just ordinary but is truly about life to the full. You'll have the very best."

The Israelites come into the Promised Land and once again fall away, so they're exiled. Yet God stays focused on his mission of bringing them to a place of goodness and abundance. He sends a Savior, and through him we can now enter the ultimate Promised Land, heaven. "To the one who is victorious, I will give the right to eat from the tree of life, which is in the paradise of God" (Rev. 2:7). The descriptions of Eden in Genesis and those of heaven in Revelation are remarkably similar. God didn't give up on his original plan when humankind fell; he just made some changes to the location.

The problem is, we tend to ignore heaven or misunderstand it. In his book *Heaven*, Randy Alcorn describes a conversation about heaven:

> A pastor once confessed to me, "Whenever I think about Heaven, it makes me depressed. I'd rather just cease to exist when I die."

"Why?" I asked.

"I can't stand the thought of that endless tedium. To float around in the clouds with nothing to do but strum a harp . . . it's all so terribly boring. Heaven doesn't sound much better than Hell. I'd rather be annihilated than spend eternity in a place like that."

Where did this Bible-believing, seminary-educated pastor get such a view of Heaven? Certainly not from Scripture, where Paul said to depart and be with Christ was far better than staying on a sin-cursed earth (Phil. 1:23). My friend was more honest than most, yet I've found that many Christians share the same misconceptions about Heaven.[1]

That kind of misconception about heaven leaves us looking for the perfection our hearts long for here, and that never works. We're left feeling weary and frustrated rather than seeing that this life is just the beginning.

You are made for a perfect place.

You are made to be a perfect person.

You are made for perfect relationships with other perfect people.

It's just not going to happen in this life.

I'm not a theologian or Bible scholar, so I'm not even going to try to get into the details of what heaven is actually like. I really don't think it's possible for us to know anyway. If God created this world in seven days and he's been working on our eternal dwelling place for thousands of years, can you even imagine what he's done? What God has in store for us will be more than our limited human minds can even comprehend right now. So while much of heaven will be a glorious surprise when we get there, I do think Scripture is clear about the *heart needs* that heaven will meet. That's the part that can help free us from seeking perfection in this life.

In Heaven You Will Fully Be Who You're Created to Be

We live in the tension of knowing we're not fully reaching our potential. And yet no matter how hard we try, it's never quite within our grasp. As soon as we resolve one issue in our lives, another pops up. Just when we think we're making progress, we discover how far we still have to go. The natural response to that is "try harder." We can turn life into a treadmill, believing one day we'll get to where we really need to be. But the reality is, we won't reach our potential until we get to heaven. Yes, we'll continually learn and grow. We're to "go from strength to strength, till each appears before God in Zion" (Ps. 84:7). But we can't complete ourselves. "He who began a good work in you will carry it on to completion until the day of Christ Jesus" (Phil. 1:6).

God created you to be who you are not just for this life but forever. You're an eternal being. Your strengths, skills, and gifts and the core of who you are will not go away when you get to heaven. Instead you will fully be who you were always created to be. I think one of the best parts of heaven will be seeing each other and saying, "Wow, you had all that in you the whole time!" Every part of you—your looks, your talents, your personality—will fully reflect the image of God when you're in heaven. You don't have to make that happen here with antiwrinkle cream and endlessly chasing empty dreams. If you try to perfect yourself in this life, you will be disappointed.

Because Scripture tells us there will be a new heaven *and* a new earth, it makes sense that we'll also put who we are to work in some way. Work has always existed, and it's part of God's character. Jesus said, "My Father is always at his work to this very day, and I too am working" (John 5:17). Work only came under a curse after the fall in Eden. And Jesus broke that curse through what he did on the cross. Work has been redeemed for us as believers and can be part of our worship. "So whether you eat or drink or whatever you do, do it all for the glory of God" (1 Cor. 10:31).

In the parable where Jesus tells about the master who entrusts his servants with talents and then goes on a journey, the reward for work isn't leisure—it's more work. "His master replied, 'Well done, good and faithful servant! You have been faithful with a few things; I will put you in charge of many things. Come and share your master's happiness!'" (Matt. 25:21). Our culture thinks "rest" is the highest goal of life. That's reflected in our pursuit of retirement and living for the weekend. But in God's eyes, work is a source of joy and satisfaction. Adam and Eve worked in the Garden. The Israelites worked in the Promised Land. And from every indication, we'll work in heaven in some way. And whatever it is will be perfectly aligned with who we are.

If you're in a job you don't love but need to do to provide for your family, you can rest assured it will not be that way in eternity. If you've put aside some of your talents for a season to raise a family, you can know you will have another opportunity to use them. If you have learning disabilities or other struggles in this life, you can know that one day you will learn and grow forever without those getting in the way of what you long to do. Your potential will one day be completely fulfilled.

Wise Solomon said, "A person can do nothing better than to eat and drink and find satisfaction in their own toil. This too, I see, is from the hand of God" (Eccles. 2:24). Work is a gift from God. And his gifts are eternal. You will not be bored in heaven. You will not get stuck singing in the choir forever. You will not sit on a cloud and twiddle your thumbs. You will live with a divine purpose that completely aligns with who you are created to be. You will work with joy, find satisfaction in what you do, and bring God glory through it.

Yes, continue to develop who you are in this life because God wants to use you as much as he can in this world. But as we talked about before, aim for excellence and not perfection. And when you feel that gap between who you are and who you'd like to be, remember God will close it forever on the day when you walk through the open gates of heaven.

In Heaven Your Relationships Will Be Perfect Too

Even in the best relationships here on earth, we're often feeling like we don't have complete intimacy. And we're right. "Each heart knows its own bitterness, and no one else can share its joy" (Prov. 14:10). As much as we may love each other and long to draw close, we're still separated by our own humanity. Because we're fallen, we incorrectly view each other's hearts. We misunderstand the motives of others. We can only partially convey who we truly are and what we're feeling. When we sense that, we feel lonely even with those people we love most. And that can lead us to believe if we can only try harder, if we can only be perfect, then we won't ever feel alone again. But that feeling is part of life, and it won't disappear fully until heaven.

I don't know specifically how it will work, but I'm certain heaven is a place of relationships. God, Jesus, and the Holy Spirit have been in perfect unity since before the world ever came into being. God is the one who said, "It is not good for the man to be alone" (Gen. 2:18). God said this *before* the fall. Relationship was part of Eden when it was a perfect place, and it makes sense that it would be part of where we live for eternity too. When you get to heaven, you will recognize the loved ones you knew here. Because like we just talked about, God doesn't wipe out who you were on earth when you get to heaven—he completes it. Since there is a new earth as well, it also makes sense that we would form new relationships while we're in heaven and go about the purpose God has for us there.

In heaven, we will have family. It won't be flesh-and-blood family like we had on earth (although we'll still know our earthly family there and have a relationship with them). Jesus talked about how the family of believers supersedes our physical family even here on earth:

> While Jesus was still talking to the crowd, his mother and brothers stood outside, wanting to speak to him. Someone told him, "Your mother and brothers are standing outside, wanting to speak to you."
>
> He replied to him, "Who is my mother, and who are my brothers?" Pointing to his disciples, he said, "Here are my mother and my brothers. For whoever does the will of my Father in heaven is my brother and sister and mother." (Matt. 12:46–50)

In a culture that often idolizes family, this can be hard to hear. Yet Jesus is clear. Once we belong to him, our "family" is about far more than flesh and blood. This should give us hope too, because none of us belongs to a perfect family this side of heaven. When the holidays don't go as planned, when there's a misunderstanding among the relatives, when a family member hurts your feelings with an insensitive comment, you can hold on to this: one day you will have the family your heart has longed for all along. And for those who have experienced far worse at the hands of family members, like abuse, you can know that you will have a fully healed and whole family forever in heaven.

When our families here let us down, our reaction is often either to try harder to be perfect ourselves or to demand that they be perfect. This leads to bitterness, distance, and broken relationships. You will never be or have the perfect daughter, mother, sister, cousin, aunt, granddaughter, or grandmother. It's impossible. Families require lots and lots of grace. The sooner we can accept that, the sooner we can enjoy the blessings the family we've been given does offer. Shred your image of the perfect family. It's an idol that will only steal your joy and make you crazy. And accept that you will never love your family or completely be loved by them in the way you'd truly like. It's not humanly possible to totally fulfill that "family" longing in this lifetime. It can only be satisfied when you join your true family in heaven. But one day that desire will be satisfied. You will have millions of believers in heaven with you who will love you as brothers and sisters. Your heart will be overflowing with feelings of belonging and of being surrounded by a family who loves you.

In heaven our family will also be our friends. On earth, those two relationships usually fall in separate categories. But in heaven they'll merge as one. You'll reunite with friends you made on earth and you'll discover new ones. Jesus said, "I no longer call you servants, because a servant does not know his master's business. Instead, I have called you friends, for everything that I learned from my Father I have made known to you" (John 15:15). We will live with Jesus as his friends forever. And we'll enjoy perfect friendship with each other.

If you've ever been hurt by your peers, felt left out, or been wounded by women—all of that will be fully healed in heaven. You will live in complete acceptance. You won't struggle with insecurity. You won't worry if you chose the right outfit. You won't strive to find the right words to convey your heart to those around you. Our fellowship with each other will be what we've longed for all our lives. Little girls seem to instinctively look for a "best friend." They imagine someone who will share their deepest dreams and highest hopes, who will be trustworthy and see the best in them, who will be like a sister even if they're not related. That's the kind of friendships I believe we'll have in heaven. If you can't find a BFF here, don't despair—you have all of eternity to do so.

In heaven and the new earth you'll enjoy the people you love in many of the same ways you do here. There will be feasts we'll go to together. You'll have a mansion created for you by Jesus where you can spend time with those you love. You'll work beside people in ways that bring everyone involved joy and God glory. You'll see other people benefit from the gifts God has placed within your heart. Close your eyes and think of everything you long for in relationships here on earth. *All of those desires will be fulfilled in heaven.* We need to know that because it frees us from expecting far too much from each other and ourselves when it comes to our connections on earth. The answer to the isolation you sometimes feel is not trying harder or making other people change. It's knowing that feeling is a homing beacon reminding you that a better place with better relationships is waiting for you. In the meantime, we are to love one another and extend God's grace to each other.

Your heart will not be lonely forever.

It will be loved forever.

In Heaven You Will Have Perfect Intimacy with God

We try to listen to God only to feel like there's a whole lot of static on the line. We study his Word to see more of who he is and walk away feeling like we still only have a glimpse. We try to follow him faithfully only to discover we're capable of straying. But one day our relationship with God will be perfect and complete. The apostle Paul describes it this way: "For now we see only a reflection as in a mirror; then we shall see face to face. Now I know in part; then I shall know fully, even as I am fully known" (1 Cor. 13:12). That verse appears in what is commonly known as "the love chapter," and that seems fitting, because when we're with God, we'll finally understand love because he *is* love.

When we're fully loved we will no longer struggle with fear, because "perfect love drives out fear" (1 John 4:18). We will never feel insecurity again. We will never struggle with thinking we're not enough. We will never distance ourselves from God out of shame. We will be able to be in his presence and know that we are completely and eternally safe and secure.

We will never be lonely again. In a mysterious way that I'll freely confess I don't fully understand, we'll be the bride of Christ. That longing for the perfect marriage, the perfect husband, will be totally fulfilled. We will be able to believe that we are a beautiful, beloved bride who is a delight to the One who loves her.

We will hear God's voice and always understand it. We won't ever have to guess what his will is or wonder if we're following it. We won't need to question if the words our hearts are receiving are from him or another source. We won't hear accusations or condemnation and worry that they're actually the voice of God trying to tell us something. We will have perfect communication with God.

We will only do what pleases God. This struggle will be over for us forever: "I do not understand what I do. For what I want to do I do not do, but what I hate I do" (Rom. 7:15). Our every thought, word, and action will bring God glory and joy. We will never sin again. We won't even struggle with temptation. We'll freely and willingly do what God wants and feel his pleasure in return.

We will grasp our true identity. When we meet God face-to-face, we'll know at once that without Jesus we could never stand in his presence. Yet we'll also fully comprehend that we have been made righteous and holy through what Christ did on the cross. We will never battle false beliefs about who we are again. We will know that we are cherished, chosen, and deeply valued.

One day with God will be better than all the ones that have come before in this life. When we stand before him we'll know, "This is what my heart has longed for all my life." God himself is the treasure of heaven. Even if nothing else were in heaven, God would be enough for us. Yet in his abundant love he adds so much more. His desire is to spend eternity with us. It still makes me shake my head in wonder as I type those words. We could never deserve for this to be our destiny, but it is. God has promised, and he will make sure all that he has planned for us comes true.

God wants us to focus on a relationship with him on earth because he knows that trying to be perfect in our behavior is not only impossible but unnecessary. If we could accomplish that, then he would never have needed to send Jesus. The moment we step from this life to the next, we will be completely perfect. And in the meantime, what Jesus did on the cross for us has already taken care of our sin. So we are to live in freedom, joy, and love—not in the pursuit of perfection. Ever since Eden, relationship and not outward behavior has always been what God desired from us. Loving God here is the purpose of your life, and it's what you'll do forever in eternity.

If you're reading this and thinking, "I'm not sure I'll get into heaven," then you can deal with that right now. The only way to get into heaven or have a relationship with God is to be sinless, and none of us can do that on our own. That's why Jesus came to earth and lived a perfect life, died for us, and was resurrected again three days later. He took our sins to the cross and paid the price for us. Now all we have to do is freely receive his gift. "If you declare with your mouth, 'Jesus is Lord,' and believe in your heart that God raised him from the dead, you will be saved" (Rom. 10:9). You can pray right now to God and say, "I believe you exist, you love me, and you sent your Son for me. I confess that I'm a sinner and I need your forgiveness. I give my life, everything I have, and all I am to you. I'm now yours forever, and I trust you to welcome me into heaven one day. Amen." You can never earn your way into heaven by being a "good person." It's only by the grace of a good God that we can spend eternity with him.

In Heaven You'll Have Your "Happily Ever After"

As little girls we grow up dreaming of princes coming for us and castles where we'll live forever. I believe there's a reason why our young hearts are drawn to those ideas. One day our prince *will* come for us and we'll live with him forever.

> Then I saw "a new heaven and a new earth," for the first heaven and the first earth had passed away, and there was no longer any sea. I saw the Holy City, the new Jerusalem, coming down out of heaven from God, prepared as a bride beautifully dressed for her husband. And I heard a loud voice from the throne saying, "Look! God's dwelling place is now among the people, and he will dwell with them. They will be his people, and God himself will be with them and be their God. 'He will wipe every tear from their eyes. There will be no more death' or mourning or crying or pain, for the old order of things has passed away." (Rev. 21:1-4)

When we picture ourselves in heaven, we tend to think of some vague, floaty existence that is completely different from what we've experienced in this life. We often miss that there will be a new heaven *and a new earth*. God isn't starting over in the passage above as much as he is bringing to completion the plan that began with Eden. He's creating a "happily ever after" for us.

> "I am making everything new!" Then he said, "Write this down, for these words are trustworthy and true."

He said to me: "It is done. I am the Alpha and the Omega, the Beginning and the End." (Rev. 21:5–6)

God has never given up on what started with one man and woman in a perfect garden. We have rebelled over and over. We have chosen sin over his ways. We have betrayed him, rejected him, and even killed him on a cross. But God is continuing on with what he always had in mind for us anyway. We love the idea of "happily ever after" because that's what we were made for all along.

When we misunderstand the longing for "happily ever after" in our hearts, we tend to react in one of two ways. Either we reject all happiness as worldly, or we demand that we be completely happy in this world. Both contribute to perfectionism.

When we reject being happy as "worldly," we believe a myth that says the Promised Land is *only* in heaven. Yes, the ultimate Promised Land is in heaven, but God wants us to thrive here too. I talk about that in *You're Going to Be Okay*:

> I flipped through the pages of my Bible until I found the story of the Israelites finally crossing the Jordan River into the Promised Land. What followed their entry didn't seem like a prototype of heaven to me. Yes, they were in the land God had given them, but there were still battles to fight, houses to build, laws to follow. Moses gives the people an intricate plan from God for enjoying life to the full in the place where God is taking them.
>
> The more I looked at Scripture, the more I became convinced: the Promised Land isn't just a representation of heaven. Instead, it's what God wants all of us to experience in this life when we live in faithful obedience to him. Yes, the *ultimate* Promised Land (what Scripture symbolically refers to as Zion) is indeed ours when we at last stand in God's presence. But to limit it to that is to miss so much of what God has for us in the here and now. . . .

Because of the myth that the only Promised Land is in heaven, it seems many Christians accept the desert as home—as the way it has to be. But that's not true. You are not made for the desert. I'm not made for the desert. God has so much more in store for us, and we don't have to wait until we die to begin receiving it![2]

The Lord "delights in the well-being of his servant" (Ps. 35:27). God desires for you to thrive in this life as well as forever in heaven. Yes, in this world you will have challenges to face. You will grieve losses. You will have hard days. But you are most certainly allowed to be happy. It's not worldly—it can even be an act of worship. When we reject all happiness, our lives become nothing more than drudgery and performance. We try to get everything right, but we end up missing so much of what God has for us. We become miserable, bitter people who are just waiting for this life to end.

We can also wrestle with the opposite: demanding to be completely happy in this world. We begin saying things like, "Well, I'm sure God would want me to do this because it makes me happy." That's because in our culture we confuse *true happiness* with *temporary pleasure*. If you have an affair, of course it's going to bring you pleasure for a while. Same goes for drinking too much, doing drugs, or eating an entire package of cookies. Our flesh will go for anything that feels good. But that doesn't mean what we're experiencing is true happiness. Happiness is an overall feeling of well-being that lasts even after that temporary pleasure is long gone. Sometimes happiness requires saying no to what we want in the moment and experiencing the pain of that so we can do what's ultimately pleasing to God and in our best interest.

Yes, God wants us to be happy. But that doesn't happen by doing whatever we want. That actually will ultimately destroy us. When we use God's desire for our well-being as an excuse for sin, we break his heart and misunderstand his love for us. To delay our happiness when necessary, we have to believe that God truly has our best interest at heart. If we don't, we'll feel that he's holding out on us or we'll justify choices that are clearly outside of Scripture. God has done everything he possibly can—even sacrificing his own Son—to make sure "happily ever after" is yours forever. "He who did not spare his own Son, but gave him up for us all—how will he not also, along with him, graciously give us all things?" (Rom. 8:32).

Both of the attitudes above can lead us into perfectionism. The first can make us reject anything we truly enjoy because we believe it must not be from God. That turns our life into nothing but work, work, work. And the second is essentially demanding life on our terms—creating our own version of "perfect" that's completely different from God's. When we understand "happily ever after" is our destiny, we can let go of both and embrace God's plan for us. The one that has been in place since Eden. The one he has never given up on. The one waiting for us in heaven.

The best moment of your life here can't even compare with what's waiting for you in heaven. All your hopes, desires, and longings will one day be fulfilled. Truly. Instead of pushing you to strive, let that craving for perfection in your heart simply be a reminder of this: *you're not home yet.*

We tiptoe around the idea of heaven because we're afraid that we won't get the details right. But that can keep us from grasping what matters most: that heaven and the new earth will hold all we wish we could have in this life. When we don't ever think about heaven, we end up trying to create our own version here on earth. Usually we do so by trying to make our relationships, our lives, and ourselves perfect. We wear ourselves out, miss the blessings we do have, and end up feeling like God is holding out on us.

When we let go of having our own heaven on earth, we can live with more courage, joy, and anticipation. We can respect the desires of our hearts rather than being frustrated by them because we understand their true purpose. We can extend more grace to those around us. We can live with a different perspective.

Heaven is real.

We're going there one day.

And if we don't get to meet in this life, I'm saving a big hug for you on the other side.

Freeing Your
Heart **Forever**

We're nearing the end of our journey together on these pages, friend. So let's walk through a final process of setting aside the pursuit of perfection in your life. These steps are intended to put into action what you've placed within your heart as you've read these pages. Think of them as declarations of your newfound freedom.

Step One: Letting Go of
Perfection in Your Past

We've all been hurt by the expectations of others. Finding true freedom means forgiving those who have contributed to the pressure you've felt to be perfect. Take time to release them to God now.

Lord,

You are a God of grace, and I'm so grateful. As fallen human beings, we don't always reflect that grace in our relationships with others. I've been hurt by these people:

_____

_____

_____

I realize that they're not perfect either, and I choose to forgive them because you have forgiven me. I understand that forgiveness is a one-time decision but an ongoing process, so I pray you will continue this healing work in my life. Amen.

Step Two: Letting Go of Perfection in Yourself

Sometimes we are harsher on ourselves than anyone else. We need to receive forgiveness for how we've wounded ourselves too, then ask God to give us a new perspective of grace.

Lord,

I have been my own worst critic many times. I've placed demands on myself that you have never placed on me. I've spoken to myself unkindly and sometimes have echoed the voice of the enemy rather than your words of love. I ask your forgiveness for that and especially for believing this lie about myself:

_____

_____

_____

I receive this truth from your heart instead:

_____

_____

Please teach me to live in grace and to truly believe that I'm loved, accepted, and delighted in by you. Amen.

Step Three: Letting Go of Perfection in Your Future

Many times when we try to be perfect, it's because we want to control the future. We think that if we just do everything right, then surely nothing can go wrong. But God alone knows what tomorrow holds, and we find peace only when we give what's coming to him.

Lord,
You are the only one who is truly in control. Sometimes I like to try to take control because it makes me feel safer. But I've learned you are my only true security and I can rest in your love for me. I've specifically been worried about these things in my future:

_____

_____

_____

While I will continue to be faithful and pursue excellence, I release the results in all of these areas to you. Please fill my heart with peace that passes understanding and confidence that you will take care of me no matter what happens. Amen.

Step Four: Letting Go of Perfection in Other People

Extending grace to others can be the hardest part of no longer chasing perfection. We can't change anyone and we're not supposed to. Only God can work in the hearts of others, and when we take a step back, it often gives him the room he needs to do so.

> *Lord,*
> *I have my own ideas about what everyone in my life should be like. I realize now those often don't line up with yours. I've tried to change people when you're the only one who truly can. So I give you the people in my life, especially my relationships with:*
>
> _____
>
> _____
>
> *Show me how you want me to be an influence in those relationships while ultimately trusting you with the lives of those I love. I will accept others as you have accepted me. Amen.*

Step Five: Letting Go of the Guilt and Shame That "Perfection" Brings

Guilt and shame always accompany perfectionism because we continually fall short. God wants to replace guilt and shame with joy and hope. You don't have to carry those burdens anymore.

> *Lord,*
> *I've struggled with guilt and shame for so long. I even sometimes thought that feeling those things was honoring to you.*

Now I understand that because of Jesus, my guilt and shame have been taken away forever. I especially release my guilt and shame about:

_____

_____

In place of guilt and shame, I receive your joy and hope. I will live with a new sense of lightness in my heart because of what you have done for me. Amen.

Step Six: Letting Go of Perfection as a Life Goal

Perfection can be highly motivating. As we move away from it, we can begin to see how much of our behavior has really been about trying harder and doing better. But God wants us to live in love instead. That is his highest goal for us.

> *Lord,*
> *I've been driven by perfection sometimes instead of led by your love. I want that to be different from now on. Thank you for freeing me from needing to do everything "just right" so I can "just be" who you have created me to be. Thank you for loving me beyond what I can even ask or imagine. I'm especially grateful to know:*

_____

_____

Your Word says, "The only thing that counts is faith expressing itself through love" (Gal. 5:6). I want to live like that's true. Thank you for setting me free to love. Amen.

Step Seven: Embracing What God Has for You Forever

God never leaves us empty-handed. When we let go of one thing, he replaces it with something even better. When you let go of perfectionism, you'll feel a void in your life for a bit. You may have been so used to being motivated by it that you feel uncertain about how to move forward. That's okay, and it's just part of the healing process. In those moments when it feels like it would be much more comfortable just to try to be perfect again, pause and ask God to help you learn to live in love.

> Lord,
> Thank you for freeing me from the pressure to be perfect. I want to live my life loving you, those around me, and myself too. I choose to believe you love me, and in response I want to say to you:
>
> _____
>
> _____
>
> You are a God of grace, and I freely receive that gift from you. I will never stop being grateful that I can have a relationship with you and even bring you joy with my life. I am yours forever. Amen.

A Final Note from My Imperfect Heart to Yours

Dear friend, I'm thinking of you wherever you are right now. I wish I could pour all of these truths right into your heart and seal them up forever. I wish I could be sure that every day you would wake up believing that you're beautiful, you're beloved, and we need what you have to offer the world. I wish I could take away every lie you've ever heard and protect you from every hurt you may face. I'd do all of that if I could.

But I know this world doesn't work that way. I know that even if you've managed to grasp some new truth on these pages, it will be hard to hold on to sometimes. I know that life is a battle and you're a warrior. I know that we're not home yet. So before we finish, I want to remind you one more time of why you really can stop trying to be perfect.

If You Try to Be Perfect, We'll Miss Out on Who You Really Are

Sweet girl, the world only gets one you. There has never been and will never be another woman who walks the earth with your strengths, gifts, and talents. You are a poem of God, a work of art, an original and not a copy. When you try to be perfect, it's always an attempt to live up to someone else's standards. And every time you do, a part of the image of God in you gets hidden. Listen to me: have the courage to be who you are. Yes, messy, mixed-up, in-progress you. It doesn't feel like it, but being who God created you to be is the best way to change the world. We don't get another chance to receive what you have to give. It either comes through you or not at all. An imperfect you is far better than you being someone else's idea of perfect.

If You Try to Be Perfect, the Law Will Win in Your Life

You are not under law but under grace. Jesus paid a high price to give you that freedom. He doesn't want you to go back to living under the law. He wants more for your life than an endless to-do list and rules. He knows those will only crush your heart and take away the joy of your relationship with him. In modern days, living "under the law" means trying to meet any set of standards in order to gain approval. They might come from your church, boss, or mother-in-law. But whatever the source, those requirements are not from Jesus. "It is for freedom that Christ has set us free. Stand firm, then, and do not let yourselves be burdened again by a yoke of slavery" (Gal. 5:1).

If You Try to Be Perfect, Others Will Feel Like They Need to Be Perfect Too

I practiced and prepared for weeks leading up to the conference. I wanted my presentation to go just right. Yet that morning it seemed God whispered, "Even if it doesn't, I can still use you." So when I had all kinds of technical trouble in the middle that even the IT department couldn't figure out, I said to the audience, "I'm glad this happened, because this is how life goes. And it's okay. We just keep going anyway." I got more comments about how that helped people than any other part of what I did. When we can embrace imperfection in life and ourselves, it makes those around us breathe a sigh of relief. We are all insecure, and we are all trying harder than we need to be. Be the courageous one who says, "I don't have it all together. But I believe we're better together."

If You Try to Be Perfect, You Won't Grow

Perfection is the great paralyzer. It will cause you to freeze up, avoid risks, and stay where you are. But that's not what God wants for you. He wants you to learn, explore, discover, and move forward. It's in the adventure of faith that we grow closer to him. We rejoice with him when things go well, and we get up and try again when they don't. God values the process of growth more than your performance. You are made for more than sitting on the sidelines of life. Go ahead and get in the middle of the action. No matter what happens, you will still be loved.

If You Try to Be Perfect, You Will Be More Likely to Struggle with Depression

The research is clear: perfectionism puts us more at risk for depression and anxiety. I know those have all kinds of causes, including physical ones, and I'm not denying or dismissing those. I just believe it's important to recognize that when we pursue perfection, we make ourselves more vulnerable to difficult emotions. Life is hard enough without our unrealistic expectations being added it to it. You can pursue excellence, enjoy your life, and receive the blessings God has for you. He wants you to thrive.

If You Try to Be Perfect, You'll Be Doing God's Work for Him

Jesus is the "perfecter" of our faith (Heb. 12:2). He's the one who will make us more and more like him over time. When we try to make ourselves perfect on our own, we interfere with that process. We can let go and simply focus on staying close to Jesus and falling more in love with him each day. You don't have to carry the burden of perfecting yourself. It's more than any of us can bear. And God already knows that you will be perfect forever one day. He's not concerned that work won't get finished in your life. He knows that because Jesus said "It is finished" (John 19:30) on the cross, one day you will be perfect when you're home with him.

If You Try to Be Perfect, You'll Miss Out on a Lot of Love

"There is no fear in love. But perfect love drives out fear, because fear has to do with punishment. The one who fears is not made perfect in love" (1 John 4:18). You have a choice to make: Will you be led by fear or by love? You can't be led by both. Yes, you will always struggle with fear in some ways, but you can decide now that it will not control you. God's love can drive out the fear in your life.

I know, friend, how hard it is to live under the burden of feeling like you need to be perfect. I've been there, and that's why I'm asking you with all my heart to believe you really are loved no matter what.

Sometimes You Will Forget All of This—And It's Okay

I finished the rough draft of this book and set it aside to marinate for a bit. In the coming weeks, I began to feel a weight press in on my heart.

"I'm tired," I confessed to friends over lunch one day.

"What's going on?" they asked.

I shrugged my shoulders and sighed. "I don't really know."

They hugged me and promised to pray I'd be filled up again.

That night I pulled out my journal, plugged headphones into my ears, and grabbed a Sharpie. I wanted to think through my life and especially my work. I began to put "Writer" at the top of the page because that's my title. But as I leaned toward the paper I felt a bit of hesitation, and I silently asked God, "What do you want me to write in that spot?" And it seemed I heard one word in response: *Worshiper*.

And suddenly I knew why I was so exhausted. *I'd switched from being a worshiper to a worker.* In other words, I'd slipped back into perfectionism. You know by now that isn't the first time that's happened to me. Like we talked about before, throughout my life when I've felt pressure mounting and expectations building,

I tend to have this heart reflex: *try harder*. Be more. Do more. Go more. I carry on like that until I get worn out and a bit rebellious.

Yes, I should have caught on a bit quicker to that pattern by now. But I'm a bit of a slow learner in this area it seems. Maybe you have one of those areas in your life too? Thankfully we serve a God of grace. A God who chases us down right in the middle of all our wild and weary-making running. A God who speaks life and peace and rest into us. A God who wants our hearts more than our hands.

I spelled out the letters slowly: "w-o-r-s-h-i-p-e-r." I crossed out these letters: "w-o-r-k-e-r." And I thought of this verse: "Better one handful with tranquility than two handfuls with toil and chasing after the wind" (Eccles. 4:6 NIV 1984). Toil is work without joy. Work that drains your life instead of filling it. And trying to catch the wind is meaningless striving. The endless doing and trying harder just to feel more in control. I'd been living both.

And God was asking me again, "Can you be satisfied with one handful?" Because here's how we're meant to live, friends: with one handful holding tight to what God has given us—love, joy, peace, grace, goodness. And the other hand empty and open for whatever else he would have us receive. Two handfuls means we're clenching our fists through life. We're gritting out teeth. We're hanging on with all our might. Two handfuls means we're tired.

Thankfully, God generously offers us what all tired people need: *rest*. Even if the world around us keeps unavoidably spinning—the toddlers keep throwing Cheerios, the projects keep coming, the calendar keeps filling—we can wrap our fingers around peace in a way that truly does pass understanding. And we can let go of all we've grasped that was never meant for us. "You can be saved by returning to me. You can have rest. You can be strong by being quiet and by trusting me" (Isa. 30:15 GW).

I filled the page with words and prayers. Then I laid my pen down. And when I laid my head down on the pillow that night too,

I felt different. Not so weary and afraid. Quieter inside. *More like a worshiper and less like a worker.* I hope to end each day a little more like that for the rest of my life, because I'm learning it's the best, most beautiful way to live. And it's ours for free.

We can all reach out and take hold of the peace that has been promised us today. And we can let go of all our striving so we can receive what's infinitely better: God's unconditional love and grace.

A few weeks after I wrote "worshiper" in my journal, I spent a weekend with some women who have shared life with me over the last year. We gathered in Branson, Missouri, and as the horizon of the city came into view, I had a realization: I had come full circle.

This city was where I spent a summer in college after my rebellious freshman year. This was the place where I first learned what grace really meant. And now I was returning again in a season where God was bringing me even deeper into that truth.

It might be reassuring if I could tell you, "I wrote a book about this, and now I will never struggle with it again." But that's not reality. What's true is that I'm far freer, more joyful, and more in love with Jesus than I've ever been before. And I hope I can say the same next week, next year, and at the end of my life. Because we are on a journey, friends. And we will continually keep learning and growing.

So if you make some progress and then discover God has even more to show you about grace, don't be hard on yourself. Instead just know that's part of being human. Don't try to be perfect at not being perfect. Amen?

When you find yourself drifting back toward old patterns, run to Jesus. With your arms open wide. As fast as you can. Just as you are. He will always be there to welcome you and remind you as many times as you need to hear it of how much you're loved and how his grace is bigger than anything you can do.

You are braver than you realize at this moment. Letting go of the pursuit of perfection is one of the wildest, most courageous things you can do in this world. It sets you free to live in truth and pursue all God has for you.

One of my favorite quotes by Jill Churchill says there's "no way to be a perfect mother but a million ways to be a good one."[1]

You can insert any word into that sentence: there's no way to be a perfect friend, sister, co-worker, follower of Jesus, but there are a million ways to be a good one. So find one little way today. Not because you have to. Not because you're worried what people will think if you don't. Not because you believe that's what it takes to earn God's approval. No, do it because you know you're truly cherished. Instead of a race, let your life become a beautiful response. You're free and you're on your way home. So enjoy the journey—even the messy parts.

There's only one thing in this world that's even better than "perfect," and that's knowing you're perfectly loved.

And you are.

No matter what.

XOXO

Holley Gerth

Go Deeper Guide
(for Individuals and Groups)

You can download a printable version of this guide for free at http://holleygerth.com/books-and-more/.

A Note from Holley

Hello, Friend!

I'm so glad you're taking time to go deeper into this book. We're all wired a bit differently, so I wanted to share some ideas for ways you can do so:

1. *Go through the questions on your own. You can write the answers below, get a printable version from holleygerth. com, or use a journal if you'd like more room.*
2. *Meet a friend for coffee and talk about a chapter each time. If you love one-on-one time, then this approach may be the best fit for you. If you and your friend don't live in the same town, you can use email, the phone, or video.*
3. *Get a group of friends together for a book club. Keep it simple. All you need is a place to meet and perhaps some snacks.*

4. Invite the women in your family to share this journey with you. Mothers and daughters, sisters, aunts, nieces, grandmas and granddaughters can all learn from each other.

5. Do the book as a study with your church, workplace, or organization. If you do, I may be able to record a brief video introduction for your group.

6. Create an online book study through your blog or a social media site like Facebook. In today's world our hearts can be together even if we live far apart.

While I hope this book has spoken to you personally, I believe these are truths that best become real through relationships. Reaching out and sharing your answers with others can take courage but it will help set you free. And by being open and willing to share, you'll encourage others too. We're in this together.

Introduction and Chapter 1: Why You Really Don't Have to Be Perfect

1. How are you *really* doing, friend?

2. When you hear the words, "You're not supposed to be perfect," what is your first response?

3. When someone asks you, "How are you?" what do you typically say? What would you really like to be able to say if you knew it would be okay to express anything you wanted?

4. When you read the "Lure of Perfection" section, what do you relate to most? Why?

5. This section says, "'For by one sacrifice he has made perfect forever those who are being made holy' (Heb. 10:14). Through Jesus, we are given perfection that we could never have on our own. That's *positional* perfection, and it allows us to stand in right relationship with God." But in our humanity we're still in the process of being made holy until that process is complete when we get to heaven. How does this idea fit or not fit with what you've always thought about what it means to be "perfect" before God?

6. In the "Let's Pause for a Minute" section, there's an opportunity to begin a relationship with God and truly give him your life. Have you done that yet? If not and you're ready to

do so, write out a prayer to him. If you have already done that, write down your faith story.

_____

_____

_____

_____

7. What has contributed to perfectionism in your life? And who has helped you understand grace and acceptance?

_____

_____

_____

Chapter 2: Embracing the Freedom That's Already Yours

1. What's something you asked your parents' permission to do as a teenager? What was the response?

_____

_____

_____

2. How do you tend to view mistakes? What's a mistake you made that helped you learn and grow?

_____

_____

_____

3. What emotions do you typically feel when you say no? What's the difference between disappointing someone and not loving them?

4. What's one way you tend to be different from most people that God has been able to use as part of his purpose for your life?

5. What would you "set down" in your life if you knew it would be okay?

6. What risk would you take if you knew you couldn't fail?

7. What other freedoms would you add to the ones shared in this chapter? "I'm grateful God has given me the freedom to . . ."

Chapter 3: Trading Guilt for Grace

1. What is the difference between guilt and godly sorrow?

2. What do you tend to feel guilty about in your life?

3. When you look at the Guilt Cycle and the Grace Cycle, which one do you most identify with? What would help you spend even more time in the Grace Cycle?

4. "Prayer and fellowship are among life's richest pleasures, but let's not stop there. Let us learn to fill our souls with beauty, art, noble achievement, fine meals, rich relationships, and soul cleansing laughter. When we acknowledge these pleasures, we acknowledge God as a genius creator of brilliant inventions. Let us be wary of a faith that denies these blessings as 'worldly' and unfit, as though Satan rather than God had designed them. Let us refuse to fall into the enemy's trap of denying ourselves God's good pleasures so that we end up deeply vulnerable to illicit pleasure."[1] When you read this quote from Gary Thomas, what thoughts come

to mind? What can you more freely enjoy that God has given you as a gift?

_____

_____

_____

_____

_____

5. Practice moving from guilt to grace with these questions:

What's a lie you've been telling yourself?

_____

What's reality?

_____

What's the real truth?

_____

6. What do you have to be grateful for and praise God about?

_____

_____

_____

7. What untrue messages have you heard about guilt? What is the truth instead?

_____

_____

_____

8. What else has God revealed to your heart about guilt and grace as you've gone through this chapter?

_____

_____

_____

Chapter 4: What Your Heart Really Needs Is Perfect Love

1. What are you afraid will happen if you're not perfect?

_____

_____

2. Only God's perfect love can rid us of our fear and free us from striving to be perfect. What lies have you believed about God's love for you, and what is really true?

_____

_____

_____

3. What messages did you receive about perfection from your father? What does God say is really true?

_____

_____

_____

4. What have friends and peers taught you about perfection? What does God say is really true?

_____

_____

_____

5. How has your husband (or your dreams about one if you're single) influenced your view of what being perfect means? What does God say is really true?

_____

_____

_____

6. How have leaders helped form your ideas about perfect performance? What does God say is really true?

_____

_____

_____

7. "People will never love us perfectly. And when they don't, it's easy to assume it's our fault. We tell ourselves, 'I'll try harder to be perfect so I can be loved.' But that's a treadmill that will lead us nowhere except to burnout and frustration." Write a prayer below telling God you're ready to get off that treadmill in any area where you may be on it and ask him to help you simply to walk with him and believe you're deeply, truly, always loved.

_____

_____

_____

Chapter 5: The God Who Loves You More Than You Know

1. How is God's love different from human love?

2. What does "being holy" mean to you? What helps you stay connected to God?

3. When was a specific time you saw or experienced God's mercy?

4. What is an area of your life where you're experiencing change and you really need for God to be your security?

5. What "cracks" in your life and heart can God pour out through this week? What are some unexpected ways he might be able to use your imperfections?

6. In the "God Is More Than We Can Even Imagine" section, which of those words are you drawn to most and why?

7. How does knowing who God is help us remember who we are and free us from trying to be perfect?

Chapter 6: Daring to Be Who You Already Are

1. Which words on the "God says you are..." list connect most with you? Why?

2. What are three of your strengths and skills?

3. "Then Jesus said to his disciples, 'Whoever wants to be my disciple must deny themselves and take up their cross and

follow me. For whoever wants to save their life will lose it, but whoever loses their life for me will find it. What good will it be for someone to gain the whole world, yet forfeit their soul? Or what can anyone give in exchange for their soul?'" (Matt. 16:24–26). What does it really mean to take up your cross when you're a believer?

_____

_____

_____

_____

4. What's your love language, and how would you describe it? I give and receive love primarily by . . .

_____

_____

_____

5. What's your sacred pathway, and how would you describe it? I connect with God by . . .

_____

_____

_____

6. What's your personality type, and which Strongest Life role sounds most like you?

_____

_____

_____

7. What's one way you can learn something new about who you are to love others and glorify God this week?

_____

_____

_____

Chapter 7: Finding Healing in Your Relationships

1. What was one of your favorite moments in school with your peers? What was one of your hardest?

_____

_____

_____

2. What's the difference between gossip and sharing about other people in a way that's helpful?

_____

_____

_____

3. Think of a time when you were criticized. How did that experience make you feel? Now think of one when you were encouraged. How did that feel different?

_____

_____

_____

4. There is no condemnation for us in Christ, and therefore we should never condemn each other. Write some words that describe the true identity we share. In Christ we are (example: loved, chosen, valued) . . .

5. Read the Commitment of Words in this chapter. What phrases in it connect most with your heart, and what else would you add?

6. Who is someone you can encourage with your words this week? How will you do so?

7. What else can women do to help each other feel safe in friendships and relationships so there's less pressure to be perfect?

Chapter 8: A Practical Plan for Beating Perfectionism

1. What's the difference between pursuing excellence and pursuing perfection?

2. What do you believe God has put you on earth to do that no one else can? (For example, no one else can be a mama to your children or create the art you do.)

3. Based on your answer above, what areas of your life are worth pursuing excellence in? What are some areas where "good enough" really is good enough?

4. What's one thing you need this week, and how can you ask for help with it?

5. What helps you live with gratitude? What are you thankful for today?

_____

_____

_____

6. What's a risk you can take this week or something new you can try that will help you learn or grow no matter what the outcome may be?

_____

_____

_____

7. Who in your life encourages you to be real, and how do they do so?

_____

_____

_____

Chapter 9: A New Perspective That Will Change Your Life

1. What's the difference between legalism and grace?

_____

_____

_____

2. How would you redefine "perfect" after all you've read so far?

    _____

    _____

    _____

3. Read Matthew 5 for context. What stands out to you in those verses?

    _____

    _____

    _____

4. "Jesus sums up all of this with the 'be perfect as God is perfect' verse. In other words, 'Be perfect not just on the outside but on the inside—in your heart.' There's only one logical response to that statement: 'That's impossible.' . . . That's exactly what Jesus wants them to realize, because he's there to tell them they need a Savior." How does this quote change the way you read the last verse in Matthew 5? What do you think Jesus is really trying to get people to understand?

    _____

    _____

    _____

5. "Let's also look at what comes right after the statement Jesus made about 'being perfect.' He follows those words up with, 'Be careful not to practice your righteousness in front of others to be seen by them' (Matt. 6:1). Jesus knows that although on one hand the people know perfection is impossible, their minds are still buzzing with new ways to

meet these requirements." What are some ways we try to make ourselves perfect in God's eyes and the eyes of others? What does he want us to do instead?

_____

_____

_____

6. When you look at the parts of perfection listed in this chapter, which one reassures your heart most? Why?

_____

_____

_____

7. What incorrect views of perfection have impacted your life? What is the truth you're ready to replace those with instead?

_____

_____

_____

Chapter 10: The Perfect Place You're Heading One Day

1. Imagine waking up in Eden. What do you think a day living there would be like?

_____

_____

_____

2. When you think of heaven, what emotions do you feel? What have you been told heaven is like?

_____

_____

_____

3. What's an area of your life where you feel you fall short of your potential? How does knowing you'll fully be who you're created to be in heaven change your perspective on that area?

_____

_____

_____

4. Who are you looking forward to being with in heaven?

_____

_____

5. What does "perfect intimacy with God" mean to you? What do you think you'll enjoy most about being with him in heaven?

_____

_____

_____

6. What does living "happily ever after" mean to you? What does your heart long for most?

_____

_____

7. How does understanding heaven help free us from the pressure to have everything be perfect in this life?

Chapter 11: Freeing Your Heart Forever

1. Who did you forgive in the "Letting Go of Perfection in Your Past" section? Forgiveness is a process. What can help you continue to forgive?

2. What's a lie you identified in the "Letting Go of Perfection in Yourself" section? What is the truth God wants your heart to hear instead?

3. What did you tell God you're giving him control of in the "Letting Go of Perfection in Your Future" section? What does God promise you no matter what happens?

4. Which relationships did you release to God in the "Letting Go of Perfection in Other People" segment? How do you think doing so might begin to change those relationships?

5. What does God want you to pursue as a life goal instead of perfection? What's one new way you can do so starting this week?

6. Which of the "If You Try to Be Perfect" statements spoke most to you? Why?

7. Even after all you've learned and the ways you've grown in grace, there will still be times you come under the pressure to be perfect again. Write a note full of love and grace to yourself that you can read again in those moments. *Dear You, I always want you to remember . . .*

Acknowledgments

A book has to be lived by the author first, so I'm especially thankful for the people in my life who have given me grace and loved me as I am.

My family—You've known me all my life and loved me at my worst and best moments. Thank you for cheering me on no matter what.

My heart sisters—We may not be related by blood, but you are family to me too. Whether you're a friend I meet locally for coffee or an online friend far away, your encouragement keeps me writing and growing.

My Revell team—You receive what I have to offer with grace and open hands, then make it better. I'm especially grateful for Jennifer Leep, Michele Misiak, Twila Bennett, Robin Barnett, and Wendy Wetzel.

My readers—Without you being here, this book would just be a Word document on my computer. Thank you so much for joining me in this journey.

My Savior—What you've done for me has set me free. I love you and will be forever thankful for your grace.

You—Wherever you are right now reading these words, I'm really glad you're here on these pages with me too.

Notes

Chapter 2 Embracing the Freedom That's Already Yours

1. Shawn Johnson, *Winning Balance: What I've Learned So Far about Love, Faith, and Living Your Dreams* (Carol Stream, IL: Tyndale, 2012), 59.

2. Malcolm Gladwell, *What the Dog Saw: And Other Adventures* (New York: Little, Brown, 2009), 37–38.

3. Larry Osborne, *Accidental Pharisees: Avoiding Pride, Exclusivity, and the Other Dangers of Overzealous Faith* (Grand Rapids: Zondervan, 2012), 203–6.

Chapter 3 Trading Guilt for Grace

1. Wayne Jacobsen, *He Loves Me! Learning to Live in the Father's Affection* (Newbury Park, CA: Windblown Media, 2007), 186.

2. Kim Sawatzky, email communication. Used by permission.

3. Gary Thomas, *Pure Pleasure: Why Do Christians Feel So Bad about Feeling Good?* (Grand Rapids: Zondervan, 2009), Kindle Location 225.

Chapter 4 What Your Heart Really Needs Is Perfect Love

1. Dr. Henry Cloud, *9 Things You Simply Must Do to Succeed in Love and Life: A Psychologist Learns from His Patients What Really Works and What Doesn't* (Nashville: Nelson, 2007), 223.

2. Ann Voskamp, "How Hurting Women Can Help Each other Heal," *A Holy Experience* (blog), April 26, 2011, http://www.aholyexperience.com/2011/04/how-hurting-women-can-help-each-other-heal/. Used by permission.

3. Beth Moore, *So Long, Insecurity: You've Been a Bad Friend to Us* (Carol Stream, IL: Tyndale, 2010), 7.

4. Stephen Arterburn and Jack Felton, *Toxic Faith: Experiencing Healing over Painful Spiritual Abuse* (New York: Doubleday, 2011), 211.

5. Emily P. Freeman, *A Million Little Ways: Uncovering the Art You Were Made to Live* (Grand Rapids: Revell, 2013), 25.

Chapter 5 The God Who Loves You More Than You Know

1. Jacobsen, *He Loves Me!*, xii.

2. Jacque Watkins, "When Mercy Found Me: Day 12: Redeemed: Part 2," *Mercy Found Me* (blog), January 6, 2013, http://www.jacquewatkins.com/2013/01/06/when-mercy-found-me-day-12-redeemed-broken-vessel-part-2/.

3. John Ortberg, *If You Want to Walk on Water, You've Got to Get Out of the Boat* (Grand Rapids: Zondervan, 2001), 27.

Chapter 6 Daring to Be Who You Already Are

1. Max Lucado, *Cure for the Common Life: Living in Your Sweet Spot* (Nashville: W Publishing, 2005), 104.

2. Paul Kroll, "Soul and Spirit in Scripture," Grace Communion International, 2014, http://www.gci.org/spiritual/soulspirit.

3. A more direct translation reads, "Love, and do what you will." Augustine of Hippo, "Homily 7 on the First Epistle of John," section 8, online at New Advent, accessed June 29, 2014, http://www.newadvent.org/fathers/170207.htm.

4. Gary Chapman, *The Five Love Languages: The Secret to Love That Lasts* (Chicago: Northfield, 2010).

5. Gary Thomas, *Sacred Pathways: Discover Your Soul's Path to God* (Grand Rapids: Zondervan, 2009), 16.

Chapter 7 Finding Healing in Your Relationships

1. Henry Cloud and John Townsend, *Boundaries: When to Say Yes, When to Say No to Take Control of Your Life* (Grand Rapids: Zondervan, 1992), 89.

2. Annie Downs, *Speak Love: Making Your Words Matter* (Grand Rapids: Zondervan, 2013), 9.

Chapter 8 A Practical Plan for Beating Perfectionism

1. Valorie Burton, *Happy Women Live Better: 13 Ways to Trigger Your Happiness Every Day* (Eugene, OR: Harvest House, 2013), 7.

2. Holley Gerth, *You're Already Amazing: Embracing Who You Are, Becoming All God Created You to Be* (Grand Rapids: Revell, 2012), 27.

3. Ann Voskamp, *One Thousand Gifts: A Dare to Live Fully Right Where You Are* (Grand Rapids: Zondervan, 2010), 155.

4. Dr. Jeremy Dean, "Practicing Gratitude Can Increase Happiness by 25%," *PsyBlog*, September 10, 2007, http://www.spring.org.uk/2007/09/practicing-gratitude-can-increase.php.

5. Margery Williams, *The Velveteen Rabbit* (New York: Start, 2012), Kindle Locations 44–46.

6. Jennifer Watson, "Hair Pulling and Tired Hands," *Broken Girl* (blog), October 16, 2013, http://brokengirl.org/2013/10/16/hair-pulling-tired-hands/.

Chapter 9 A New Perspective That Will Change Your Life

1. Gerth, *You're Already Amazing*, 131.

2. Ibid., 46.

3. Allison Van Dusen, "How Depressed Is Your Country?" *Forbes*, February 16, 2007, http://www.forbes.com/2007/02/15/depression-world-rate-forbeslife-cx_avd_0216depressed.html.

Chapter 10 The Perfect Place You're Heading One Day

1. Randy Alcorn, *Heaven* (Carol Stream, IL: Tyndale, 2004), 5–6.

2. Holley Gerth, *You're Going to Be Okay: Encouraging Truth Your Heart Needs to Hear, Especially on the Hard Days* (Grand Rapids: Revell, 2014), 116–77.

Chapter 11 Freeing Your Heart Forever

1. Jill Churchill, *Grime and Punishment* (New York: Avon, 1989), 1.

Go Deeper Guide

1. Thomas, *Pure Pleasure*, Kindle Location 225.

About Holley

Holley Gerth is a bestselling author who loves sharing God's heart for women through words. She does so through books like *You're Already Amazing*, as a life coach, and through partnerships with companies like DaySpring.

When she's not writing, Holley loves spending time with her husband, Mark, having coffee with girlfriends, and finding ways to keep learning and growing, because we're all a beautiful work in progress.

Holley would love to hang out with you at her place online (www.holleygerth.com).

Connect with
Holley at
HolleyGerth.com

We can all encourage each other—
one prayer, one word,
one act of kindness at a time.

You truly care. You want to help others. You love giving
encouragement. But you aren't sure what to pray, what to say,
or what to do. Take courage! You already have what you need
most: a loving heart. And now Holley Gerth shares
simple ways to turn your care into action.

"Holley Gerth turns words like a poet. Warm and personal, *You're Already Amazing* is a biblical, practical handbook for every woman's heart."

— Emily P. Freeman, author of *Grace for the Good Girl*

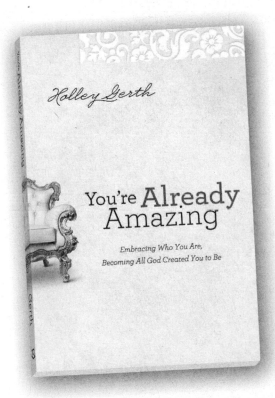

With this heart-to-heart message, Holley Gerth invites you to embrace one very important truth—that you truly are already amazing. Like a trusted friend, Holley gently shows you how to forget the lies and expectations the world feeds you and instead believe that God loves you and has bigger plans for your life than you've ever imagined.

Revell
a division of Baker Publishing Group
www.RevellBooks.com

Discover the dreams God has given you—
and then dare to pursue them.

Holley Gerth takes you by the heart and says,
"Yes! You can do this!" She guides you with insightful
questions, action plans to take the next steps, and most
of all, the loving hand of a friend.

 Revell
a division of Baker Publishing Group
www.RevellBooks.com

Available Wherever Books Are Sold
Also Available in Ebook Format